Tourism and Travel

ISSUES

Volume 222

Series Editor

Lisa Firth

Independence

Educational Publishers

Cambridge

First published by Independence

The Studio, High Green

Great Shelford

Cambridge CB22 5EG

England

© Independence 2012

Photocopy licence

The material in this book is protected by copyright. However, the
purchaser is free to make multiple copies of particular articles for instructional
purposes for immediate use within the purchasing institution.
Making copies of the entire book is not permitted.

British Library Cataloguing in Publication Data

Tourism and travel. -- (Issues ; v. 222)

1. Tourism--Social aspects. 2. Ecotourism. 3. Volunteer

tourism.

I. Series II. Firth, Lisa.

338.4'791-dc23

ISBN-13: 978 1 86168 607 7

Printed in Great Britain

MWL Print Group Ltd

CONTENTS

Chapter 1 Travel Trends

Chapter 2 Sustainability and Ethics

OTHER TITLES IN THE ISSUES SERIES

For more on these titles, visit: www.independence.co.uk

A note on critical evaluation

Because the information reprinted here is from a number of different sources, readers should bear in mind the origin of the text and whether the source is likely to have a particular bias when presenting information (just as they would if undertaking their own research). It is hoped that, as you read about the many aspects of the issues explored in this book, you will critically evaluate the information presented. It is important that you decide whether you are being presented with facts or opinions. Does the writer give a biased or an unbiased report? If an opinion is being expressed, do you agree with the writer?

Tourism and Travel offers a useful starting point for those who need convenient access to information about the many issues involved. However, it is only a starting point. Following each article is a URL to the relevant organisation's website, which you may wish to visit for further information.

Overseas visitors to Britain

Understanding trends, attitudes and characteristics.

Five key insights

⇨ The UK is the sixth most-visited destination by international tourists but is losing market share.

⇨ Built heritage, cultural heritage and contemporary culture are core to Britain's offering, with shopping and watching sport popular activities.

⇨ Britain is a vital cog in the global aviation network, but competitor destinations across Asia and the Middle East are investing heavily in expanding their own connectivity and aviation infrastructure.

⇨ Tourists are increasingly demanding authentic experiences and are going the extra mile to find value for money; user-generated web content underpins this trend.

⇨ Outbound travel from countries in developing parts of the world is growing rapidly, but international travel is primarily intra-regional rather than inter-regional, so western European markets continue to offer growth potential for Britain's inbound visitor economy.

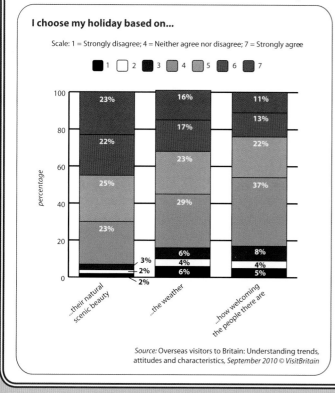

Source: Overseas visitors to Britain: Understanding trends, attitudes and characteristics, *September 2010* © VisitBritain

Tourism trends

Global tourism declined in 2009, with 40 million fewer international tourist arrivals than in 2008 on the back of the global economic slowdown, but the basic facts remain the same; as a destination Europe accounts for roughly half of all international tourism, and four-fifths of these trips are intra-European. Asia Pacific is the fastest growing region for inbound and outbound tourism in relative terms, but there is a long way to go before volumes start reaching European levels, and what's more, nine in ten Asia Pacific international tourism trips are intra-regional – the long-haul outbound market from this part of the world will become increasingly important, but its role for British tourism should be seen in the correct context.

The UK is the sixth most-visited destination by international tourists

Outbound markets often described as 'mature' can still offer huge growth potential. With the ongoing implementation of the Western Hemisphere Travel Initiative in the US the proportion of US adults owning a passport now stands at 33% (94.5 million) according to Donald N Martin & Company, with figures from US authorities showing that in the year to September 2009, 11.9 million new or renewal passports were issued.

It is hard to see any reversal of the trend towards more destinations emerging on the radar; in the 1990s it was all about Prague and Budapest, over the past decade it has been Marrakesh and Dubai and in the years ahead Libya and India will grow in importance when thinking about which destinations Britain is competing with for international, and for that matter, domestic tourism. In 2009 most destinations saw a decline in international tourist arrivals, but the list of some of those that enjoyed growth (admittedly often from a low base) is telling; Turkey, South Africa, Cuba, Peru, Cambodia, Bahrain, Montenegro and Morocco.

The increasing marketing 'clout' of more established players in trying to attract inbound tourism represents

VISITBRITAIN

a further threat, with the likes of Tourism Ireland and Tourism Australia having invested heavily in marketing.

Motivations and attitudes to holidays

Increasingly, research shows that holidays are no longer seen as a luxury in life, but as a necessity for many to escape the stresses of everyday life and unwind. It is therefore not surprising to see that 'taking vacations in my own country' is seen as the eighth highest priority in people's lives on average. Taking domestic holidays is at least 'quite important' for 74% and 'extremely important' for 15%.

Further evidence that a balanced life is more highly sought after in 'developed' nations emerges when looking at the importance of 'having time to relax'. This was amongst the top three priorities in Australia, Canada, Germany, Italy, Japan, Korea, Sweden, the UK and the USA but a slightly lower priority (sixth or lower) in many emerging economies such as Brazil, Egypt, India, Mexico, Russia and Turkey.

One way that many people seek to relax and achieve more balance in their lives is through holidays. Indeed, there is a widely reported growing trend towards 'wellbeing' holidays, although this remains a relatively niche opportunity at present...so where do holidays feature as a priority in life?

Foreign holidays are seen as at least 'quite important' for 60% of online respondents, with 11% saying they are 'extremely important'. Most of the surveyed nations say that domestic holidays are more important than foreign holidays, with three exceptions: the UK, Germany and Russia. The UK and Germany are the two largest source markets for outbound tourism in the world, so it is no surprise to see the emphasis they place on foreign holidays. Russians' aspiration to visit other countries highlights the potential growth that could be achieved from this emerging economy under the right conditions. 75% of Russians see foreign holidays as at least 'quite important', with 44% saying they are at least 'very important' and 16% 'extremely important'.

Other countries such as China, Egypt, India, the USA and Japan place a far lesser importance on foreign holidays – just 34% of Japanese respondents regarded them as 'quite important' and only 3% as 'extremely important'.

For most people, taking foreign holidays linked to their religion is not regarded as particularly important. Just 7% of respondents saw this as 'extremely important'. For all nations surveyed apart from one, taking foreign holidays linked to their religion was ranked 17th (lowest priority). The exception was Egypt, who reported that foreign holidays linked to their religion (14th) was a higher priority in life than general foreign holidays (17th). This reminds us that it is always important to understand local attitudes towards holidays.

Holiday influences

70% of respondents agreed they choose destinations based on their natural scenic beauty, highlighting the importance of showcasing Britain's natural assets to the best of its ability to appeal even more widely. Although Britain's natural beauty is often seen positively by overseas residents, Britain is ranked just 24th out of 50 nations in the Nation Brands Index (2009) for its natural scenic beauty – clearly showing that there is very strong competition from other nations here.

One area where Britain is seen as a truly world-class destination is in terms of its history and culture. History and culture are strong influencers of holiday destination choice (57% agreed), so Britain is in a strong position to capitalise here, being ranked as the fourth best nation in terms of its culture in the NBI and fourth in terms of its built heritage.

62% agreed that they like to see famous and well-known locations on holiday, but 66% like to explore new places, so it is important that Britain can cater for both these needs.

The Chinese, for example, are particularly keen on seeing famous locations (72% agree) on their travels, so it is important to include iconic imagery such as Big Ben in marketing materials to reassure them that they are not going to miss out on the 'must-see' attractions. More mature markets such as Australia want to get beneath the surface of destinations a bit more, getting away from the crowds (71% agree), so highlighting authentic cultural experiences (e.g. pubs) and 'hidden gems' (whilst maintaining an element of the 'must-see' attractions) is important.

36% agreed that films they had watched have influenced their choice of holiday destination, whilst 33% disagreed. For music, only 24% agreed it had influenced their choice and 43% disagreed. Younger age groups are more likely to say that films (43% agree) and music (33% agree) have influenced their choice of holiday destination than older age groups.

It is also essential that Britain meets the emotional needs of consumers; twice as many agree it is more important that holidays are exciting than relaxing (42% agreed and 21% disagreed), but clearly Britain should be able to visibly cater for both needs. Younger visitors agree more strongly than older visitors that holidays should be exciting (47% of 18-24s and 25-34s agree compared to 34% of over 55s). The USA, Japan and China are least likely to be looking for an exciting break. Indeed, Japanese respondents were twice as likely to disagree (34%) than agree (16%) that 'it is more important that holidays are exciting than relaxing'.

46% regard welcoming people to be important when choosing a destination, so it is also important to show that Britain is a welcoming nation to potential visitors.

Booking travel

The Internet is seen as a safe way to book travel more often than not, with more agreeing (45%) than disagreeing (18%), although there is a certain amount of variation in different markets, so it is always wise to check individual markets before assuming that the Internet will be trusted.

Countries like Sweden (59%), the UK (60%) and the USA (61%) are far more likely to see the Internet as a safe way to book travel than countries such as Egypt (27%), Russia (38%) and Brazil (30%).

> *History and culture are strong influencers of holiday destination choice (57% agreed), so Britain is in a strong position to capitalise here*

Using a travel agent for holiday bookings is a useful alternative for many with 34% saying they prefer to use an agent, although 29% disagreed. Many markets still rely heavily on travel agents, and many travellers have strong relationships with them. 44% of Japanese agreed they prefer to use a travel agent to book holidays and just 13% disagreed. Likewise, 59% of Russians said they prefer to use an agent, with 15% disagreeing.

Travel behaviour

From the majority of countries around the world, outbound travel is largely intra-regional; approximately three quarters of outbound trips involve travel to another country in the region. It is therefore not surprising to see that more people say they prefer to take lots of short breaks rather than fewer long breaks (38% agreed and 25% disagreed).

25% of respondents agreed they were experienced international travellers, whilst 48% disagreed. Not surprisingly, nations with a high propensity to travel abroad were most likely to agree they were experienced, such as the UK (41%), Sweden (40%) and Germany (29%), whilst other nations such as Brazil (12%), Egypt (18%) and Japan (10%) were less likely.

Whilst it may be easy to understand why nations such as Brazil and Egypt do not regard themselves as experienced international travellers, Japan is one of the largest outbound travel markets in the world, with around 20 million outbound journeys each year. However, one must also consider that Japan is a nation of 127 million people, so one might expect it to be an even larger outbound market. One of the key features of travel from Japan has been the trend away from long-haul travel. Whilst travel from Japan to other Asian destinations has shown some growth since 2000, travel to Europe and the Americas has declined significantly.

Amongst all nations surveyed, most respondents indicated they are not averse to travelling long distances; only 21% agreed that it is too much effort to travel for more than five hours for a holiday. However, the Japanese were more likely to agree than any other nation, 29% doing so.

September 2010

⇨ The above information is an extract from VisitBritain's report *Overseas Visitors to Britain*, and is reprinted with permission. Visit www.visitbritain.org for more information.

© VisitBritain

VISITBRITAIN

Why tourism matters

This article sets out why tourism matters so much to Britain's economy, its potential for rapid and balanced economic growth, and the Government's goals for the sector as a whole.

It's big...

The size and importance of tourism in the UK's overall economy is often underestimated. It's our third highest export earner behind Chemicals and Financial Services. In most years it's the fifth or sixth biggest sector of our economy, behind manufacturing and retail but ahead of construction. It generates £90 billion of direct business for the economy each year, contributes £115 billion to GDP when you include the supply chain and £52 billion directly and is one of our biggest employers, with over 200,000 businesses providing 1.36 million jobs or 4.4% of all employment.

⇨ Domestic tourism accounts for 59% of the sector's spend, while inbound travellers account for 14% and outbound 27%.

⇨ Britain consistently ranks as one of the top six or seven visitor destinations in the world, and because of our open and international economy, business travel is an important (and high spending) element of both our domestic and foreign travel sectors too.

⇨ We're comparatively weak in the lucrative international business conventions and conferences market, but are improving rapidly as large and modern new facilities such as ExCel in east London come onstream.

⇨ In our leisure travel, we used to take package holidays abroad but are becoming increasingly self-confident and adventurous, so we're increasingly likely to 'self-package' instead – often online.

⇨ We've always self-packaged our domestic holidays, partly because we're more confident about what we're buying and partly because package holiday firms' economics work best if you're flying to your destination, so they're naturally a much smaller part of the domestic market.

⇨ We're taking more frequent, shorter breaks than we used to. And, finally...

⇨ We're much more likely to holiday abroad, and less likely to take a domestic break, than other European nationalities.

Balanced...

Equally, because we have so many excellent tourist destinations scattered across the country, the sector offers great opportunities to rebalance the UK's economy away from its historic over-reliance on finance, construction and the south-east. This means tourism should be a strong contributor to delivering the Government's strategy for local growth set out in the White Paper *Local Growth: realising every place's potential.*

Creates new jobs...

Tourism is particularly labour intensive compared to many other sectors of our economy, so the industry is very effective at creating more than its fair share of jobs as it expands. British tourism is expected to employ 1.5 million people directly by 2020, and 2.9 million if indirect employment (mainly amongst suppliers to the industry) is included. Equally importantly, the sector delivers a wide and well-balanced range of jobs and careers; it creates jobs at every skill level, in both full-time and part-time employment, in all corners of Britain.

Boosts regeneration...

Tourism is a particularly effective vehicle for regenerating run-down neighbourhoods, using relatively small amounts of new investment to revitalise existing assets. In rural areas this means our beautiful coast and countryside; in urban neighbourhoods it could be disused waterfronts, iconic buildings or revitalised cultural venues such as museums and art galleries too. The leverage effect isn't limited to physical assets either – festivals and cultural connections can be equally powerful. For example, the Straw Man Festival in Fenlands, *Dr Who*'s association with Cardiff Bay and Liverpool's association with The Beatles have all been key elements of local regeneration success stories. This ability to leverage existing assets makes the visitor economy a particularly financially-efficient motor for regeneration. Compared to other sectors of the economy it requires relatively little initial funding, which then acts as a catalyst for further inward investment. Relative to other approaches it needs comparatively fewer high-cost capital projects with long lead times.

...and something more

Finally, tourism provides something extra which few other industries can offer: an opportunity to showcase our country's great heritage and national assets in a way

which doesn't just delight our visitors but also improves our everyday quality of life. It's not just that a good place to visit is usually a great place to live – although that's often true – but that, if we live somewhere which is beautiful and impressive, and which the rest of the world wants to visit, it gives us something to be proud of too.

March 2011

⇨ The above information is an extract from the Department for Culture, Media and Sport's report *Government tourism policy*, and is reprinted with permission. Visit the DCMS website at www.culture. gov.uk for more information on this and other related topics.

Britons to spend £7 billion on home holidays this summer

Information from BigHospitality.

The British tourism industry is set to receive a £7.2 billion boost this summer from cash-strapped Britons opting to take their holiday break in the UK, reveals a new travel study conducted by the budget hotel group Travelodge.

The survey of 5,000 British adults conducted earlier this month found that 35 per cent of respondents will be holidaying in the UK this summer, compared to 25 per cent last year.

And with the average seven-day UK holiday expected to cost £422.69 (down £144.31 from 2010), Travelodge estimates that the sector will benefit by an additional £7.2bn from summer 'staycations', or home holidays.

'It has been a tough year for many British adults with rising household costs and Government cutbacks, but our research shows that cash-strapped Britons are clinging onto their annual holiday in order to add some cheer into their lives,' said Shakila Ahmed, Travelodge spokesperson.

'Due to hefty financial cutbacks, more Britons are opting for a "staycation" break this year, which is great news for the British tourism industry.'

Top UK locations

The report found that 41 per cent of respondents are finding it more difficult to make ends meet this year compared to last year, which means they are postponing their holiday bookings until the last minute. Instead of booking holidays in January, most people will be booking in June, July and August.

'Britons are definitely waiting [until the] last minute to book their Staycation break this summer, as we have seen a rise in summer bookings following the royal wedding weekend,' said Ahmed.

'Top locations are Cornwall, Devon, UK capital cities as well as the coastal locations such as Blackpool, Brighton, Scarborough, Eastbourne and Bournemouth.'

The top ten holiday 'hotspots' for UK tourists are:

⇨ Cornwall

⇨ Lake District

⇨ Devon

⇨ London

⇨ Edinburgh

⇨ Scottish Highlands

⇨ Wales (North and South)

⇨ Blackpool

Holiday expenses

The survey found that most Britons are planning three short UK breaks this year.

Out of those taking a summer break, one-third will be opting for a seaside holiday, while one-quarter will go for a city break.

A further 22 per cent will be taking a rural holiday, 20 per cent will be visiting relatives and ten per cent will opt for a theme park-based holiday.

Out of the average staycation expenses of £422.69, the majority (£232.23) will be spent on travel and accommodation (down £20 from 2010), while a further £172.23 will be spent on visiting attractions (an increase of £67.23 from 2010).

When quizzed why they were choosing a British break this year, 38 per cent of respondents said it was cheaper than going abroad. The average foreign break is thought to cost £1,427.58.

23 May 2011

⇨ The above information is reprinted with kind permission from BigHospitality. Visit www.bighospitality. co.uk for more information.

DEPARTMENT FOR CULTURE, MEDIA AND SPORT / BIGHOSPITALITY

Brits will spend a fifth less on 2011 holidays

78 per cent of Brits say price is most important factor when booking holidays.

Hard-up Brits may be feeling the pinch, but when it comes to getting away the majority aren't prepared to give up their holiday, according to research from travelsupermarket.com. The poll of over 2,000 adults[1] revealed that just 11 per cent of Brits definitely won't be going on holiday next year – slightly up on ten per cent last year. However, the amount they are prepared to spend on their main holiday has fallen considerably – by nearly a fifth.

A year ago the average Brit was prepared to spend £1,014 per person on their main holiday, but fast forward to 2011 and this has dropped to £829. The research indicates a clear shift in spending habits amongst Brits – six months ago 43 per cent identified cost as a key factor when booking their holiday, but this figure has now surged to 78 per cent. It now towers over the traditional importance of weather (37 per cent) and facilities (37 per cent) when it comes to the 2011 getaway.

The research, the fourth bi-annual poll commissioned by travelsupermarket.com, includes a Holiday Spending Money Index, which found that current weekly spending levels (not including flights and accommodation) are also down three per cent on July 2010 from £307 to £298. And there is a continued dependence on credit cards – seven per cent will be relying on the plastic for spending money compared to six per cent last year.

It appears that when it comes to the sexes, women are watching the wallet a little more carefully – although both men and women are budgeting less than they have previously. Of those who do budget, men will take an average of £334 a week per person, down from £348 six months ago, but still well above the figure from a year ago which was £313. For women, the figure is steadily decreasing – they are budgeting £258, which is down from £265 six months ago and £278 a year ago.

Those from Northern Ireland are still the biggest spenders, budgeting £373, an average of £40 more than the nearest region – London. However, this is down from £420 six months ago. Those in the Midlands appear to be the most frugal, with those in the East Midlands budgeting £256 and West Midlands £273.

And when it comes to the overall holiday, men are slightly happier to flash the cash – they are prepared to pay on average £922 per person for their main summer holiday compared to £740 for women. Those in the south-east are prepared to spend the most on their main holiday (£960) closely followed by Londoners (£950).

Perhaps surprisingly, despite recent holiday company collapses, the misery caused by the ash cloud and all the issues snow has presented in recent weeks, the number of people who ensure their holiday is Air Travel Organisers' Licensing (ATOL)-protected has gone down from 21 per cent six months ago to just 18 per cent.

Bob Atkinson, travel expert from travelsupermarket.com, said: 'It appears that when it comes to luxuries, holidays are one thing Brits simply aren't prepared to give up. In

order to get away however, a whopping three-quarters of Brits will be looking for deals and best value as their key determining factor when booking a holiday.

'Pre-holiday research is the key – invest a bit of time in investigating to see what good deals or added extras are out there. It's certainly encouraging to see that 47 per cent of Brits shop around to get the best deal when it comes to travel – but the real question is why aren't the other 53 per cent?

'And with all the unrest in the holiday industry I'm shocked that more people still don't see ATOL as important when booking their holiday. Even if you get the cheapest deal in the world, you could still lose it all if something happens to the company.'

Bob Atkinson's top money-saving tips

⇨ Set yourself a maximum budget – considering both your spending money and the cost of booking travel and accommodation, try and stick to it and don't stretch yourself too far financially.

⇨ Do lots of online research – on your favourite holiday companies, airlines and travel sites and compare offers on a price comparison website such as travelsupermarket.com as you may be able to find companies that you have not heard of with an even better deal.

⇨ Focus on the final price for your holiday – when comparing offers and deals, how much will you pay today and how much will the deposit be? Don't just focus on the discount message and any freebies. Is it within your budget guidelines?

⇨ Don't rely on the 'freebies' – if considering a package holiday with free child places, ensure you get a price with both a free place and also a second quote without a child price. Sometimes 'free' places can cost more due to extra charges tour operators make for under occupancy.

⇨ Beware of low deposit deals – you often have to pay the remainder of the full deposit within only a few weeks, so it is only an introductory offer from many companies as opposed to a genuine long-term saving.

⇨ Think about your board basis – all-inclusive holidays allow you to set your budget here in the UK and keep a check on extras when away. Self-catering will allow you to make and prepare your own food and avoid eating out – great when you have small children to cater for. Or choose hotels on B&B, half board or full board.

⇨ Think about where you plan to go – what is the cost of living like? Will you be able to get away with a smaller amount of spending money or will you need to dig deep for cash in more expensive destinations?

⇨ Consider where you stay – it may be cheaper outside of the city or resort: however, you may end up paying more for taxis and travelling around to and from the beach or attractions. Book somewhere that has good access to public transport. If hiring a car, check you have somewhere to park close to your accommodation that won't cost a fortune.

⇨ Book before it goes – when you get a price and a deal you are happy with, book it. Prices for holidays, flights and hotels can change quickly so don't miss out on a cracking deal. It is unlikely that a cheaper deal for exactly the same holiday will come along once you have done a full check of availability.

⇨ Check your deal has ATOL cover – if it doesn't then ensure you have full protection insurance from your holiday company that covers all elements of the booking, or take out travel insurance immediately with 'End Supplier Failure' in case anything goes wrong with the company, airline or hotel you are booked with. Pay by credit card or Visa debit card where possible for additional protection.

⇨ Use a price comparison site to compare prices on package holidays – travelsupermarket.com has a revamped search that allows you to leave the destination open to get an idea of prices across many destinations; once you have a destination you can use the date tab at the top to see if it is cheaper travelling up to three days either side of your requested date; and on the results page you can use filters to check out, for example, if a 4-star hotel is cheaper than a 3-star, or narrow the results down to one of your favourite brands.

⇨ Don't forget to budget for all those extras – airport parking, transfers, car hire and baggage costs; the earlier you book, the more you save.

Note

1   Travel comparison site travelsupermarket.com is conducting a six-monthly poll of over 2,000 people called the Consumer Travel Barometer, the first of which was in July 2009. It's an ongoing tracker of Brits' views on holidays and travel. The barometer is a snapshot of British attitudes to holidays – to go away or not to go away, what type of holiday, where to go and how much to spend.

25 January 2011

⇨ The above information is reprinted with kind permission from TravelSupermarket.com. Visit www.travelsupermarket.com for more information.

© *TravelSupermarket.com*

Planes, trains and smartphones: trends affecting adventure travel in 2011

The following excerpts from recently published studies are intended to provide a snapshot of what media and mainstream research firms are talking about regarding the travel industry. We start with shifts in the Middle East...

By Nicole Petrak

Middle Eastern boom

It's no secret that the Asian market is fuelling the global tourism recovery, but, joined with an increasing number of visitors from the United Kingdom, they may be turning the Middle East into one of the world's fastest-growing hotspots.

In September, OAG reported that Dubai International Airport has surpassed JFK in flight and seat capacity, reflecting the popular rise of Dubai holidays in both Europe and Asia; meanwhile, the region also experienced steady airline growth from Latin America, the Asia Pacific, and from North America. Egypt, Turkey and Dubai have long been popular destinations for Europeans, but now as more travellers come to explore, they're increasingly shifting out to new areas.

> **Traditional voluntourism destinations, such as many Sub-Saharan African communities, are beginning to see a decline in tourist numbers**

EasyJet, the UK's largest airline, will be taking advantage of the new EU Open Skies agreement by offering roundtrip flights to Jordan beginning in March 2011 for only £106. Abu Dhabi, Syria and Tunisia are also seeing more travellers and are expected to ramp up their tourism infrastructure throughout the year.

Shifts in voluntourism?

The buzz around the growth of voluntourism continues, with Western consumer interest in volunteer trips anywhere between one-half and one-quarter of all respondents to surveys completed by companies like Tripadvisor, Conde Nast and msnbc.com. According to Peter Yesawich, CEO of YPartnership, a leading US hospitality marketing agency, 6% of all US active travellers took a volunteer vacation in 2009. Even companies like the Ritz Carlton have been getting into the voluntourism game at some locations, showing that even affluent travellers are feeling the need to get involved and give back.

Yet even as the niche grows, there's been increasing coverage in the media that voluntourism is, at best, tokenism, and at worst, exploitation of the destination's locals. Other reports relay travellers who've come home unhappy after struggling with overly rigorous work programmes or experienced exacerbated cultural clashes instead of a better understanding. Because of this, it is ATN's prediction that there will be more industry focus in 2011 on programme planning, marketing and client preparation among all sectors.

Voluntourism.org also reports that some traditional voluntourism destinations, such as many Sub-Saharan African communities, are beginning to see a decline in tourist numbers due to increasingly unaffordable costs of university volunteer programmes or the personal expenses of footing the bill for several months of living in another country, as well as from the increased media attention on the potential harm short-term volunteer tourism can do in, say, an AIDS orphanage. These trends could suggest that there is an increase in more local voluntourist initiatives, as well as a shift from aid-centric programmes to those in sustainable development, which continues to be a main focus across industries.

A deeper look at sustainable tourism

The 2010 WTM *Industry Report* found that over a third of senior travel industry executives think 'environmentally aware' holidays will be the biggest consumer trend through 2015. ABTA Travel Association predicts tour operators will increasingly participate in certification schemes and give consumers more ethical choices when marketing their trips in 2011, and that consumer focus will be on development projects in host destinations, water conservation, and ethical treatment of tourism workers and host communities who have been negatively affected by tourism influxes.

However, *ITB World Travel Trends Report* predicts a more discerning eco-consumer with the LOHAS (Lifestyles of Health and Sustainability) traveller as the new premium tourism customer, with anywhere from five to 30% of Western populations falling into this movement of 'well-off, well-educated, health-conscious and socially and environmentally aware' people. Comprised of a diverse sub-group with similar attitudes, the LOHAS mindset goes beyond the typical green consumer. Analysts have found them to be open-minded, globally cognisant and actively looking for travel that is socially ethical and environmentally sustainable; they are increasingly aware and critical of greenwashing practices. ITB points out that the US ecotourism market alone is estimated at $42 billion.

Price remains the top factor with these travellers, followed by sustainability concerns, and only then, brand names. ITB reports that 60% of the LOHAS group sees CO_2 compensation as unsustainable, while efficient energy use and waste management and a focus on local community as suppliers were rated most important.[1]

Planes, trains and automobiles via netbooks, iPads and smartphones

65% of senior executive members think booking vacations with new technologies is the most important consumer movement for the coming years.[2] The same study found that almost 60% of UK consumers who relied on social media sites for travel information did not book their original vacation after consulting their social media communities, with more than a third changing their hotel choice, and 12% switching the country they planned to travel to. Women (74%) and consumers over 55 (80%) were more likely to use TripAdvisor for these decisions, while men (42%) and 25- to 34-year-olds (52%) utilised Facebook.

> *Almost 60% of UK consumers who relied on social media sites for travel information did not book their original vacation after consulting their social media communities*

Yet ITB maintains that despite the high adoption of social media sites, their use for travel purchase decisions is still at an early stage, with only 20% of people forgoing more traditional websites for the same purpose. Establishing trust, credibility and dependability now is the most critical component as travel suppliers move into social media marketing, along with segmenting social media targets by type and positioning products with a targeted image, with a focus on metrics.[1]

Meanwhile, smartphones are stealing the limelight, with as many as 40% of international travellers already utilising them. More than 40% of these consumers access destination information on them, and 26% of leisure travellers make booking changes on them while en route; 37% of international travellers access social networks on their phones, posting photos, blogs and feedback while still at the destination.[1]

The competition for travel apps is just getting started, with both big players within the industry (TripAdvisor) and big players outside it (Wikipedia's iPhone app Wikihood) already dominating the game. Augmented reality applications – which use the phone's GPS, camera and compass to overlay images and data for the consumer when they view their surroundings – are popping up in mobile applications offerings (such as Lonely Planet and the Dutch Tourism Board).[1] More consumers are using apps that provide real-time travel information, such as TripIt and Trip Deck, to manage reservations, connections and track flight and transportation changes as they happen. Facebook Places and Foursquare are among many popular applications that allow people to find out where hotspots are and see where others are 'checking in', while a host of other apps (Fwix, Goby) help people locate events, deals, groups of common interests and ratings of places.

Notes

1   *ITB World Travel Trends Report 2010/2011*

2   WTM *Industry Report*, 2010

6 January 2011

⇨ The above information is reprinted with kind permission from the Adventure Travel Trade Association. Visit www.adventuretravelnews.com for more information.

You've booked your plane ticket, accommodation, organised travel insurance and looked up all the cheap eateries... all that on your phone?

Really...where's your sense of adventure?

Lucky for me there's an app for that too!

ADVENTURE TRAVEL TRADE ASSOCIATION

Travel health advice from Dr Felicity Nicholson, Trailfinders Travel Clinic

Stay healthy on holiday this season.

Introduction

When it comes to going on holiday, most holidaymakers finish their planning once they find their passport. However, new research has revealed that we need to become savvier when it comes to thinking about our holiday health. We forfeit travel insurance for magazines at the airport and often don't consider any health issues that could arise while we're away.

With large numbers of people travelling further afield to more exotic locations in search of sun and adventure, the need to think about staying healthy is even more important.

New research has shown that Brits are seriously unprepared for their holidays

Travel tips

New research[1] has shown that Brits are seriously unprepared for their holidays, especially when it comes to considering their health. Six in ten adults have admitted to falling ill whilst on holiday, which is unsurprising as health comes in at the bottom of the list of concerns after being robbed (27%) and the flight crashing (23%). Concerns about different food, water or environment mean the top destinations Brits perceive as high risk are Africa (19%), India (18%) and Pakistan (14%). In reality, the top three places where holidaymakers fall ill are Spain (32%), Greece (14%) and France (9%). Over 40% of UK travellers experience travellers' diarrhoea each year, making it the primary health problem encountered while abroad. A bout of this can be costly in terms of both days lost on the sun lounger or exploring your destination of choice, but also money from associated medical costs – particularly in more severe cases. To help protect you and your family from travellers' diarrhoea, Trailfinders Travel Clinic has these top tips to ensure a happy, healthy trip abroad:

⇨ Avoid tap water unless you are 100% sure it is safe to drink. This applies to ice cubes, washed salads and when brushing teeth. If unsure, drink only bottled water with a sealed lid.

⇨ Use antibacterial gels and wipes to clean your hands before eating.

⇨ Take Bimuno prebiotic before you travel to build up your immune strength and digestive protection.

⇨ Ensure you eat well-cooked meat and eat it whilst it's hot.

⇨ Avoid shellfish and other seafood if it is not properly cooked.

⇨ Only eat fruit that you can peel yourself.

⇨ Avoid food exposed to flies.

Note

1   Research conducted March 2011 on behalf of Bimuno by 72Point, with 3,000 UK adults.

⇨ The above information is reprinted with kind permission from Dr Felicity Nicholson. Visit www.bimuno.com for more information.

Is Britain an attractive tourism destination?

An extract from the Department for Culture, Media and Sport's report Government Tourism Policy.

The most important factors for tourists choosing a holiday destination are the country's weather; its natural beauty; whether it offers value for money; the quality and warmth of the welcome which visitors receive, and whether there are plenty of interesting cultural or heritage things to do while they're there. These factors are consistent over time, and don't vary appreciably for tourists from different countries either, so they explain the choices of UK holidaymakers deciding where to take their annual holiday as readily as travellers from Italy, USA or Russia. There are, however, important variations and patterns within the overall picture:

⇨ Tourists don't need every holiday to provide all these elements, particularly if they visit more than one destination each year. Many people will happily take a short break to a destination with unreliable weather, for example, if they've already spent a week sunbathing on a beach earlier in the year.

⇨ Some segments of the market have distinctly different priorities depending on their stage of life and interests. For example, on average, 20-somethings are more likely to take short breaks to visit music festivals like Glastonbury, Reading or Leeds while middle-class professionals are often more interested in visiting castles, museums and art galleries.

⇨ Geographical and cultural proximity matter more than this ranking shows. It's both cheaper and more convenient to visit somewhere which is easy to reach from home and, for nervous or inexperienced travellers, experiencing an environment which is less 'alien' is more enjoyable too. So most sunseekers from Europe go to Mediterranean countries, for example, while those from the USA or Canada go to the southern USA or central America. Of course, some types of travellers demonstrate the importance of these factors in precisely the opposite way, by deliberately seeking out places which are as out-of-the-way and different from home as possible. But either way it underlines the importance of these criteria.

So, if these are the most important criteria for persuading visitors to choose the UK, how are we doing? Data shows that the UK is definitely a successful and attractive visitor destination, for foreign and domestic travellers alike, and that we've earned our overall top six ranking across a broad range of criteria. The problem is that four of the five most important criteria – the weather, value for money, natural beauty and welcome – are where we earn our lowest scores. The UK only really shines on one of the top five: culture and heritage. This shows the enormous attractive power of our castles, museums, art galleries and festivals – many of which are free – but it's still a relatively narrow and potentially fragile foundation for such an important part of our economy and, crucially, leaves us vulnerable to new tourist developments in other countries. Competition from new heritage destinations (think of Cambodia with Angkor Wat, Peru with Machu Picchu or China with the Great Wall, the Terracotta Army and the Forbidden City) is growing massively and can only get tougher in future too. As a result, we can't rely solely on our culture and heritage to maintain Britain's ranking as an attractive tourist destination. Broadly, the recommendations in [the Government Tourism Policy] paper are intended to strengthen our visitor economy's performance in the other key areas where we're relatively weak, to ensure we maintain and improve our position as one of the world's best countries to visit, no matter what.

⇨ The above information is an extract from the Department for Culture, Media and Sport's report *Government Tourism Policy*, and is reprinted with permission. Visit www.culture.gov.uk for more.

© Crown copyright

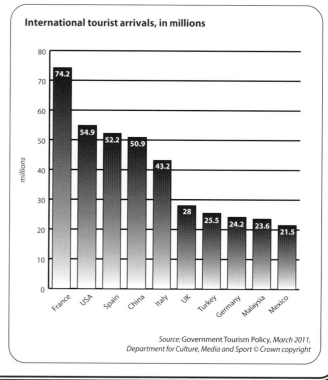

International tourist arrivals, in millions

Country	millions
France	74.2
USA	54.9
Spain	52.2
China	50.9
Italy	43.2
UK	28
Turkey	25.5
Germany	24.2
Malaysia	23.6
Mexico	21.5

Source: Government Tourism Policy, March 2011, Department for Culture, Media and Sport © Crown copyright

DEPARTMENT FOR CULTURE, MEDIA AND SPORT

£3 million from Olympic budget to boost domestic tourism in 2012 and beyond

Ensuring economic legacy for the whole country.

Three million pounds from the Olympic budget is to be used to boost domestic tourism in 2012 and beyond, in a drive to maximise the economic legacy of the London Games for the whole country.

The investment, announced today by Culture Secretary Jeremy Hunt, will kick start a new tourism campaign to make the most of the Torch Relay and the Cultural Olympiad to showcase the whole nation. Over the next three years it is expected to deliver:

⇨ 12,000 new jobs;

⇨ £500 million extra tourist spending;

⇨ 5.3 million more short break nights taken;

⇨ ten per cent additional overnight short breaks.

Secretary of State for Culture, Olympics, Media and Sport Jeremy Hunt said:

'London's Olympic Games are a part of the Government's drive to boost the country's economy and have already delivered a huge economic legacy. Businesses up and down the country have already benefited from the 75,000 Olympic contracts awarded, but we need to do more. The whole country is paying for the Games, and I want to make sure that the whole country benefits.

welcome. We are delighted to be working alongside the Government to ensure the full potential of the Olympics, the Diamond Jubilee, the Cultural Olympiad and all the events of 2012 are realised by the tourism sector across the country through the delivery of a joint marketing campaign with industry.

'Our research shows that people have been taking more holidays at home and enjoying the great experiences on offer. 85% of respondents to our satisfaction survey described the destination they visited as excellent or good and 86% would recommend it to others. It is essential to use 2012 to reinforce this trend and strengthen the future of tourism, thereby supporting the economy and employment.'

On top of the Government's £3 million from the Olympic budget, VisitEngland will contribute a minimum of £2 million, with match funding from the private sector to bring the total to at least £10 million.

12 September 2011

⇨ The above information is reprinted with kind permission from the Department for Culture, Media and Sport. Visit www.dcms.gov.uk for more information.

© Crown copyright

£3 million from the Olympic budget is to be used to boost domestic tourism in 2012 and beyond

'The UK has a wealth of stunning destinations on offer, whether it's a weekend in Yorkshire or a night on the Norfolk Broads, and I want us all to re-discover the wonderful attractions on our doorstep. The Olympic Torch Relay and the Cultural Olympiad will shine the spotlight on some of the most amazing parts of our country. It will be a fantastic opportunity for those areas to sell themselves to the world, boosting their local economies and creating jobs.'

VisitEngland CEO James Berresford commented:

'The announcement today of £3 million from the Olympic budget to boost domestic tourism is extremely

UKinbound warns against Olympic 'misperceptions'

With just one year to go until the start of the London Olympics 2012, UKinbound has warned against 'misperceptions' that it be viewed as good news for the inbound tourism industry.

Mary Rance, Chief Executive, UKinbound said:

'We are now just one year away from the London Olympics 2012. The countdown has begun and the surge in media hype and political posturing that seems to revolve around every Olympic Games will begin. Rightly so, as it is a tremendous event that brings any nation into the sharp focus of the world's population.

'However, before the International Olympic Committee (IOC) and media bandwagons roll into London, placing us centre stage in the global media spotlight, I would like to draw attention to a few misperceptions amongst politicians, the media and the wider public.

'Next year's momentous event is not the "London" Olympic Games. It is in fact the IOC Olympic Games that happens to be taking place in London – and that, from an inbound tourism viewpoint, is a massive difference. The people that will flock into London and other parts of the UK for the Games will not be traditional inbound tourists – they will be IOC enthusiasts who are primarily fans of the Olympics and will, in many cases, only attend the Games. The lack of affordable accommodation in London for those wishing to book in advance is also a key deterrent and area of concern.

'Indeed, many of my members, who represent a cross section of businesses who are reliant on inbound tourism including tour operators, other service providers such as attractions, restaurateurs, ticket agencies and transport providers, are forecasting a downturn in business for summer 2012. Even if many concede that the global media coverage and focus on London and the UK will create a positive impression, few see any immediate benefits to their business from the Games, and those that do, see the opportunities as limited in the run up.

> **The people that will flock into London and other parts of the UK for the Games will not be traditional inbound tourists – they will be IOC enthusiasts**

'The real threat to the inbound tourism sector is that of "displacement" with visitors being put off travelling, not just to London but elsewhere in the UK – and not only in 2012, but perhaps, more worryingly, 2013 and beyond. This makes the quality and performance of our transport infrastructure, the prices of hotels, food, beverages et al, all the more vital to the long-term welfare of Britain's third most important export revenue generator – inbound tourism.

'Key factors that deter potential visitors from coming to the UK also need to be addressed in order to avoid losing out on the potential positive media portrayal of London and the UK that the London Olympics 2012 might generate – these are punitive Airport Departure Taxes, high rates of VAT on accommodation and other services, and cumbersome visa application processes in key emerging markets such as China.

'In this next year our industry would like to hear politicians and media discuss the event in terms of being a springboard for 2013 and beyond rather than falling for the misperception that the IOC Olympic Games is, in itself, good for inbound UK tourism.'

26 July 2011

⇨ The above information is reprinted with kind permission from UKinbound. Visit www.ukinbound.org for more information.

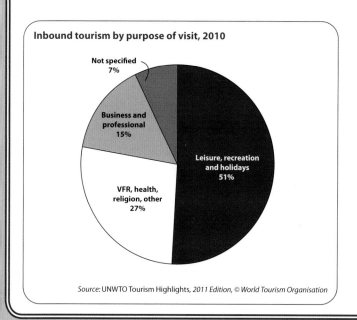

Inbound tourism by purpose of visit, 2010

- Not specified 7%
- Business and professional 15%
- Leisure, recreation and holidays 51%
- VFR, health, religion, other 27%

Source: UNWTO Tourism Highlights, 2011 Edition, © World Tourism Organisation

UKINBOUND

Raising air passenger duty flight tax will hurt UK tourism, Osborne told

George Osborne's plans to push up air passenger duty by around ten per cent is driving foreign tourists away and undermining David Cameron's Great Britain campaign, tourism chiefs have warned.

In a letter published in *The Daily Telegraph* today, senior figures in the travel industry have voiced fears of the damage the rises, planned by the Chancellor, will do to the British economy.

An increase which should have come into force last March was deferred, but the small print of the last budget made clear that this increase in APD, which is linked to the Retail Price Index, will be implemented on top of the 2012 increase.

It will add about ten per cent to the tax. A family of four taking a transatlantic flight, for example, will have to find another £24 on top of the £240 they already pay in APD.

There are fears that the rises will not only hit British families planning holidays abroad, but also put off incoming tourists who pay the tax on their flights home.

> ## A family of four taking a transatlantic flight, for example, will have to find another £24 on top of the £240 they already pay in air passenger duty

This could have major implications for the economy, according to the letter, which has been signed by the heads of the British Air Transport Association, the Airport Operators Association, UK Inbound and the Association of British Travel Agents.

'The vast majority of organisations involved in the inbound tourism industry would much rather see the Government address the significant financial barriers tourists face when coming to the UK.'

'Britain already has by far the highest levels of aviation taxes in the EU,' continues the letter. 'In two month's time the Chancellor is expected to announce substantial air passenger duty rises.

'This will further deter inbound tourism, the value of which has already dropped by more than six per cent in the last year.'

The inflation-linked rises, which would add around ten per cent to the cost of flying, is not the only levy in the offing for air passengers.

In January the European Union will be implementing an Emissions Trading Scheme, which will see airlines have to pay if they exceed their 'carbon ration'.

Some industry experts believe that this could add an additional £10 to the price of a transatlantic fare.

Airlines who support the ETS scheme believe that it should replace APD, rather than supplement it.

'An increase of ten per cent in APD is the last thing the industry needs,' said Simon Buck, chief executive of the British Air Transport Association.

'This will do huge damage to tourism and put us at a competitive disadvantage. The Government should be phasing it out.

'With passenger numbers not rising as fast as the Government forecast, there is a danger future tax rises could be even higher to make up the shortfall the Treasury is now facing.

'That would be a final and almost fatal blow to the entire tourism industry.'

The proposed rises were also condemned by a Virgin Atlantic spokesman.

'The UK already has one of the highest air taxation regimes in the world, with a family of four travelling to Florida forking out £240 in air passenger duty alone. This obviously has a huge impact on the affordability of

THE TELEGRAPH

a family holiday, but is also stifling the economic growth that the country badly needs.

'With the additional cost of the Emissions Trading Scheme coming into force next year, the Government must make air passenger duty more internationally competitive. The Chancellor could start by cancelling his plans for a double-inflation increase in April 2012.'

But Richard Dyer, Friends of the Earth's aviation campaigner, called on Mr Osborne to stand firm.

'The Government should make the aviation industry pay its fair share – it's shocking that it still gets away without paying fuel tax or VAT and highly polluting freight planes remain untaxed.

'UK aviation emissions have more than doubled since 1990 – we need to keep them under control to protect us all from dangerous climate change and an increased passenger tax is one way of doing this.'

Meanwhile, APD on long haul flights from Northern Ireland is to be reduced from £60 to £12 from November. The change, which will also see the tax on premium cabins reduced from £120 to £24, is intended to protect Belfast's service to New York and enable the airport to compete with the Republic of Ireland, where rates are considerably lower.

28 September 2011

Foreign Office releases figures on Brits in trouble overseas

The number of Britons arrested overseas has fallen by over 10%, but despite this positive trend Foreign Office staff still handled 5,700 arrest cases last year.

Though down by 20% overall, drug arrests continue to be a significant problem for some countries, particularly parts of South America and the Caribbean where a high proportion of total arrests are drug-related.

Foreign Office Minister David Lidington said:

'We work hard to warn British nationals about the consequences of breaking the law abroad so it is really encouraging to see the overall number of cases of arrests and drug arrests falling. But last year there were still 5,700 arrests of British nationals overseas. Prison conditions in some parts of the world can be very poor, overcrowded and, in some cases, dangerous and sentences can be much tougher than in the UK. People are mistaken if they think the Foreign Office can get you out of jail. We can't, but we will work hard to try and ensure your safety, and that you get a fair trial.'

Foreign Office research reveals that:

➪ 43% of 18- to 24-year-olds know someone who has taken illegal drugs whilst abroad. It also showed that two-thirds of people in Britain don't always find out about the laws of the country they are visiting before they go abroad – putting themselves at risk of unknowingly breaking the law.

➪ Nearly a third (32%) of people are not aware that they will always be prosecuted under local law if they break the law abroad – with 6% of people thinking they will be prosecuted under UK law, 22% thinking it depends on the country they are in and 4% admitted to not knowing at all.

Aside from arrests, the *British Behaviour Abroad* report published today shows that the number of Brits hospitalised abroad has increased to 3,752 cases, despite fewer people from the UK travelling abroad last year. Medical treatment abroad can be very expensive and to avoid being faced with large bills if taken ill or after having an accident, the Foreign Office is urging people to take out a comprehensive travel insurance policy before they go away this summer. Previous research suggests that 15% of Britons travel abroad uninsured.

Other key findings:

➪ Spain continues to be the country where most Britons require assistance (4,971 cases) but when you take visitor and resident numbers into account, you are most likely to need consular assistance in the Philippines, Thailand and Pakistan.

➪ The number of rape cases in Greece almost halved since 2009/10 from 27 to 15, although the numbers of sexual assault cases rose significantly.

➪ The number of Brits hospitalised abroad has increased, with Spain handling the most cases (1,024), followed by Greece. Proportionally, Brits are most likely to be hospitalised in Thailand.

➪ In total, Foreign Office staff handled 19,228 serious consular cases last year.

4 August 2011

➪ The above information is reprinted with kind permission from the Foreign and Commonwealth Office. Visit www.fco.gov.uk for more information on this and other related topics.

THE TELEGRAPH / FOREIGN AND COMMONWEALTH OFFICE

Five types of alternative tourism

Blog post from the HotelClub Travel Blog.

By Florin Nedelcu

For some people, a week on a cruise ship or at an all-inclusive beach resort is pure torture. Others prefer museums and a posh hotel over a hike through a national park. Ecotourism? Sounds like a great way to get a snake bite. For others, however, absolute heaven.

The point, of course, is to illustrate that diverse catalysts compel us to travel. Different reasons motivate different people to leave home and explore the world. With that expressly in mind, here are five types of alternative tourism.

Disaster tourism

Disaster tourism' is somewhat of a paradox. In the name of self-preservation after all, most people flee from natural disasters. A slim, intrepid minority, however, prefer to fling themselves into the eye of the storm, as it were, or show up to observe the aftermath. Less aid workers and more storm chasers, these adrenaline fiends just like to watch.

Some notable disaster tourism sites include South Asia and South-East Asia after the Indian Ocean earthquake and tsunami of 2004, New Orleans and the US Gulf Coast post-Hurricane Katrina, and the 2010 Eyjafjallajökull eruption in Iceland.

Dark tourism

The name is self-explanatory but to expound further, dark tourism is travel to some of the most sombre and grim historical points of interest on the planet. Think sites of unspeakable horror, like the Auschwitz-Birkenau concentration camps in Poland, Khmer Rouge 'Killing Fields' of Cambodia and Robben Island off the Cape Town coast.

Other noteworthy dark tourism destinations include Ground Zero in New York City, the American Cemetery and Memorial in Normandy and Hiroshima Peace Memorial Park. Yad Vashem in Jerusalem, Rwanda's Murambi Genocide Museum, Goree Island off the coast of Dakar, Senegal, Ghana's Cape Coast Castle and the International Slavery Museum in Liverpool also embody this austere, yet vital and significant, type of travel.

Ghost tourism

A fascination with the supernatural drives some people to travel in search of the paranormal. Behind many a famous landmark is a great ghost story and indeed, popular tours in places like Dublin, St. Augustine, Florida, Quebec City and Brisbane explore historic, 'haunted' city quarters.

Offshoots of 'ghost tourism' include proverbial ghost towns, from barren mine, mill and railroad towns across America, Canada and Australia to notorious places like Jonestown, Guyana and Chernobyl, Ukraine. Salem, Massachusetts, of infamous witch trial fame, and parts of Transylvania also fit the bill.

Slum tourism

One of the most controversial types of travel involves tours of vast urban slums in places like Rio de Janeiro, Soweto, Mumbai, Manila, Cairo and Mexico City. 'Shanty tourism' or 'poverty tourism' is certifiably questionable and on the ethical borderline when the experience is utterly passive. If, however, visitors engage in some kind of community outreach or volunteer programme, the collective positive impact falls beyond the realm of mere 'slum tourism'.

From the favelas of Rio to Orangi Town, Karachi, Khayelitsha township in Cape Town to Cité Soleil, Port-au-Prince, the major slums of the world do manage to lure tourists. Is slum tourism inherently good or bad? The answer is complex and elusive. Ultimately, if areas of dire poverty incur some immediate net benefit, the pros may outnumber the cons. If, however, this alternative form of travel veers on cheap voyeurism, then we can safely call it like it is: inhumane.

Pop-culture tourism

Pop-culture tourism, unlike some other types of travel, is, by definition, harmless fun. Simply put, it involves destinations with indelible connections to popular books, films, television shows, music, major events or a particular celebrity.

Countless fans of The Beatles who flock to Liverpool hotels safely fit the description of pop-culture tourists. Vulcan, Alberta, so named in 1915 after the Roman god of fire, shot to cult-like prominence decades later because of *Star Trek*. The diminutive Canadian town now ranks as a famously kitsch sci-fi pilgrimage point.

Other significant pop-culture destinations include the town of Burkitsville, Maryland (of *Blair Witch Project* fame), the Tatooine *Star Wars* sets of Matmata, Tunisia and last but not least, parts of New Zealand that evoke Peter Jackson's *Lord of the Rings* visions of Middle Earth.

⇨ The above information is reprinted with kind permission from the HotelClub Travel Blog. Visit http://blog.hotelclub.com for more information.

Brits for blast off: tourists head to final frontier

A company director from Yorkshire and a property developer from Surrey are among the ordinary Britons set to enjoy Sir Richard Branson's astro-tourism, reports Philip Sherwell in New Mexico.

By Philip Sherwell

They are the Britons who are preparing to boldly go where no tourist has gone before – and now they have all had their first sight of the VSS Enterprise, the spaceship that will take them there.

This was not *Star Trek*, but the launch pad for the world's first venture taking fare-paying passengers on a joyride into space.

Some 460 people from almost 50 countries are queuing up to glimpse the world seen from space, 70 of them from Britain

Among the 15 future British space travellers who had travelled to a remote corner of the New Mexico desert in America were a former Olympic canoeist, a professional astronomer, a businessman and his yoga-teacher girlfriend.

All are stumping up $200,000 (£125,500) for the opportunity to be among the world's first space tourists, when Sir Richard Branson's Virgin Galactic company begins taking travellers outside the Earth's atmosphere late next year.

After the inaugural flight – on which Sir Richard intends to take his two adult children plus three other guests – some 460 people from almost 50 countries are queuing up to glimpse the world seen from space, 70 of them from Britain.

'I was always fascinated with everything about space, from exploring the universe to looking for aliens,' said Craig Burkenshaw, 41, a travel company director from Doncaster. 'But until this opportunity came along, I had accepted that there was no way I'd have a chance to go into space in my lifetime. I had written off that dream.'

Some 150 signed-up would-be passengers witnessed the unveiling of the first purpose-built commercial spaceport last week – a futuristic vision of glass and steel rising out of the scrub.

The celebration marked the start of the final countdown to civilian space travel, and many passengers also had their first glimpse of the spacecraft that will carry them 70 miles above Earth.

'It seems a bit surreal to be here in the desert and realise this is really going to happen,' said Ronan McCarthy, 42, a property developer from Richmond, Surrey.

'I've got an adventurous streak, but I don't even like turbulence that much, so I do sometimes wonder what I'm doing hurtling into space.'

In a series of swooping fly-bys, Dave Mackay, the British chief test pilot, steered the 'mother vessel' – a giant plane with the VSS *Enterprise* attached beneath – over the Lord Foster-designed edifice, a jaw-dropping sight for those watching.

To make a spaceflight the *Enterprise* will detach itself, high in the atmosphere, and fire its own rocket to launch itself beyond, into brief sub-orbit.

For Jon Goodwin, a retired businessman from Newcastle-under-Lyme, it was a magical sight. 'That was the moment it really sunk in – that I will be going into space in the near future,' he said.

The 68-year-old has canoed, cycled and motor-rallied his way across some of the remotest spots on Earth, from the Atacama Desert in Chile to the Himalayas, since selling his family's wholesale confectionery and tobacco business 13 years ago. He paid his $200,000 up front in 2005.

'I am an adventurer and this is the greatest adventure,' said Mr Goodwin, a former Olympic canoeist. 'I am as fascinated by speed as space. I own ten Ferraris and they can do zero to 60 in five or six seconds. So the idea of travelling at 2,500 mph just blows my mind.'

Nigel Henbest, 60, from Princes Risborough, Buckinghamshire, who studied at Cambridge under the Astronomer General and has written 37 books about the universe, shared the elation. 'This was quite simply one of the most fantastic days of my life,' he said, still beaming several hours later. 'I have just visited the world's first commercial spaceport and seen the spaceship and it really brought home that I will be going into space soon. The beauty and simplicity of the scene was overwhelming.'

THE TELEGRAPH

Mr Burkenshaw said he had harboured the same dream since he watched the first Shuttle launches as a schoolboy. 'I think that soon people will be going into space for $50,000, which really is like buying a new car.' His girlfriend, Joanne Le Bon, 37, a yoga teacher, sceptical at first, has now caught the buzz and signed up too.

For now, the spaceship is being put through its paces at a former US air force base in California's Mojave Desert. A major test of the rocket is set for early December and the first trial flights into space are expected to begin early next year.

> ## To make a spaceflight the Enterprise will detach itself, high in the atmosphere, and fire its own rocket to launch itself beyond, into brief sub-orbit

Sir Richard hopes to take his daughter Holly and son Sam on the inaugural flight – with a few minutes of weightlessness at its peak – before the first intrepid tourists follow.

'We owe the next step in man's exploration of space to the passion of these pioneers,' the Virgin chief said as he gave an impromptu tour of the spaceport's interior. From the entrance, he led *The Sunday Telegraph* across an elevated corridor, with glimpses down into a cavernous hangar that will house the spaceships, and into the astronaut lounge where giant curved windows offer spectacular views across the 10,000-ft runway and the distant San Andres mountains.

'The building is out of this world, which is of course what it's meant to be,' he said.

The showman had earlier abseiled down the façade with Holly and Sam, smashing a bottle of champagne against the glass and naming it the Virgin Galactic Gateway to Space. Among the cheering guests were Princess Beatrice, whose boyfriend Dave Clark works for Virgin Galactic, and Kate Winslet, whose new boyfriend is Ned Rocknroll, Sir Richard's nephew and another employee of the business who changed his name by deed poll from Smith.

Several celebrities have put their money down to fly. Comedian Russell Brand, *Dallas* star Victoria Principal, film director Bryan Singer, designer Philippe Starck, scientist Professor Stephen Hawking, property developers the Candy brothers, and PayPal founder Elon Musk are all reported to be among the passenger list.

'My approach to life is to dream and set seemingly impossible challenges and then try and surround myself with people who make them become reality,' said Sir Richard. 'In 20 years' time, I hope that people will be at the stage where they are thinking: "Shall we go into space or go the Caribbean for our holidays?"'

But at least one Branson is unconvinced by the lure of space – his wife Joan. Sam and Holly said that their mother was nervous about seeing her husband and two children all take the first trip together.

'Of course, she's right to have concerns about safety,' said Sir Richard. 'I have concerns about safety. That's why we're only going to fly when we are absolutely sure it's safe.'

23 October 2011

THE TELEGRAPH

South Africa – top destination for structured gap year programmes

Information from the Year Out Group.

For the fourth year in succession South Africa has topped the list as the most popular destination for structured gap year programmes according to research carried out by Year Out Group, the association of leading gap year organisations. Thailand quickly recovered its place in the top ten once the security situation returned to normal, while Ecuador is the only South American country to feature in the list and India has gained ground.

Richard Oliver, Chief Executive of Year Out Group, comments, 'South Africa's enduring popularity stems from the diverse nature of the country and the availability of a wide range of suitable and worthwhile projects. These projects range from conservation work in the many public and private game parks, a variety of teaching placements, many opportunities to coach sports, and volunteering in health centres and orphanages including HIV/AIDS awareness programmes. These projects can last from a few weeks to a whole year. South Africa is also seen as a comparatively safe destination, there are plentiful flights and the cost of living is good value.'

Canada has consolidated its position in the top three. There are now several more organisations offering winter sports activities including ski and surfboard instructor courses that invariably lead to offers of paid work as an instructor on completion of the course, which is an attractive proposition in difficult economic times. For those that wish to venture further into the mountains there is now the possibility to train as a mountain leader. The companies are also making good use of the facilities in the summer months: as mountain biking increases in popularity so does the demand for instructors and the Canadian countryside provides the ideal testing ground to gain the necessary skills and experience.

India is gaining in popularity as discerning British and international students and graduates seek to learn more about this rapidly developing country. There is no better way to experience the culture of a country and learn about its customs than to take up a voluntary work placement. The longer the placement, the greater the understanding gained and the more beneficial the experience for both the volunteer and the host organisation.

Thailand has always been a popular gap year destination but it dropped out of favour in 2009 owing to the poor security situation in Bangkok and many other parts of the country. As it happened, no placements had to be cancelled because of the troubled situation and all were available throughout, but safety is an important factor when planning a gap year and many of those considering a gap year while the troubles were in the press decided to steer clear of Thailand and go elsewhere. Now the country is back in favour.

Currently the situation in North Africa and the Middle East is not affecting gap year projects as these areas have not traditionally been popular destinations. The main factor affecting those planning a gap year is cost and particularly the cost of flights, and the impact of additional taxes on flying especially. It will be interesting to see if this affects the popularity of Fiji, Australia and New Zealand when this survey is conducted again next year.

4 July 2011

⇨ The above information is reprinted with kind permission from the Year Out Group. Visit www. yearoutgroup.org for more information.

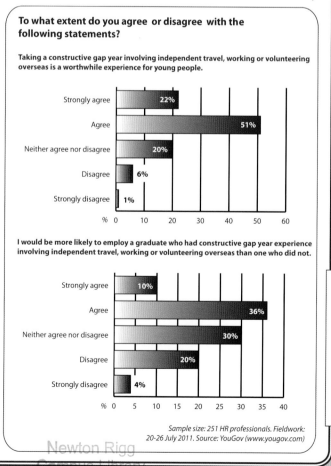

To what extent do you agree or disagree with the following statements?

Taking a constructive gap year involving independent travel, working or volunteering overseas is a worthwhile experience for young people.

Strongly agree	22%
Agree	51%
Neither agree nor disagree	20%
Disagree	6%
Strongly disagree	1%

% 0 10 20 30 40 50 60

I would be more likely to employ a graduate who had constructive gap year experience involving independent travel, working or volunteering overseas than one who did not.

Strongly agree	10%
Agree	36%
Neither agree nor disagree	30%
Disagree	20%
Strongly disagree	4%

% 0 5 10 15 20 25 30 35 40

Sample size: 251 HR professionals. Fieldwork: 20-26 July 2011. Source: YouGov (www.yougov.com)

YEAR OUT GROUP

Glamping – camping at its best

Camping has never looked so good. More comforts than home, luxurious furnishings in beautiful surroundings with plenty to keep the children happy and a fridge to cool the wine. It definitely is time to take a new look at camping and many accommodation providers have done just that.

Glamping or upmarket camping is certainly experiencing a boom, becoming more widespread and more varied. With everyone looking for value-for-money holidays, combined with staying closer to home and a better awareness of environmental issues encouraging us to get back to nature, camping has become a great solution that ticks all the boxes. It seems to fit the times we live in, highlighting the key elements of a successful holiday – scenic location, a bit of luxury, a bit of adventure but without being too cost-prohibitive.

It is not surprising, then, that according to the Visit England UK Tourism Survey, between 2006 and 2009, the AB category participating in camping and caravanning holidays grew from the smallest customer segment to the second largest. Camping has moved up in the fashion stakes. In 2009, UK residents took 18 million camping and caravanning trips, spending £2.5 billion during their trips, according to the UKTS Visit England Tourism Survey. By contrast, they made 10 million visits to Spain. In 2009, camping and caravanning trips by UK residents grew by 20%, ahead of overall domestic holiday growth of 17% (UKTS).

In the UK there are is a whole host of options under the heading Glamping – which seems to have moved up another level to encompass the likes of Iron Age Roundhouses in Cornwall, yurts, safari-style tents complete with oven and fridge, Ekopods, wigwams, tipis and authentic gypsy caravans. Celebrities have helped to make camping 'cool' as various A-rated stars are spotted on camping holidays and designer brands are producing ranges of retro-chic glamping accessories to make things look like magazine shoots.

Holland is also seeing an upsurge in Glamping holidays, which has been reflected in the offering at this year's Vakantiebeurs Travel Fair, held in Utrecht. 'We have definitely noticed an increase in exhibitors offering this type of product at Vakantiebeurs this year, it is becoming increasingly popular as a holiday option in Holland – especially in the de Waddeneilanden region. Suncamp are one of the better-known operators offering upmarket camping in Holland and are very active in the sector of luxury camping,' says Dagmar Ypenberg-Moonen, Exhibition Manager.

Although upmarket camping has been on the horizon for a while now in the UK market, this is not necessarily so in all European markets. Portugal, Spain and France have a good range of locations to offer but Northern Europe is not yet as active. Per Magnusson, Exhibition Manager for TUR in Sweden, says the trend is still very new in Sweden but he expects to see it grow in importance on the exhibitor listing in the near future.

In 2009, camping and caravanning trips by UK residents grew by 20%, ahead of overall domestic holiday growth of 17%

If you want to find out more about what is on offer around the world, Goglamping.net is probably the leading source on luxury camping, where you can find details on a range of stunning holiday options in countries from Cambodia to Chile. The directory lists venues by location or type and gives a short description of each, listing key features along with prices and a direct website link. In Goa, a hybrid tent-house, known as a 'touse', can cost from €450 per week, and in contrast The Resort at Paws Up, Montana, USA offers the ultimate in glamping: luxurious tents complete with camp butler at $715 per night for two.

It may be taking a while to reach some countries but the time is ripe for glamorous camping and there is opportunity for hotel chains and accommodation providers to add an outdoor option to their portfolio. Countries such as those in the Middle East, where families enjoy nights under the stars in the cooler months, are perfect locations and destinations such as Dubai are already known for their upmarket hotels and luxury lifestyles. The Al Maha Resort, which opened in 1999, was the first eco-tourism project to open in the Arabian Gulf but the time may now be right for hoteliers to take that next step and offer similar luxury under canvas.

Camping may not be for everyone but it is most definitely not the arduous, second-rate holiday option that it once was. The opportunity to experience being at one with nature whilst still having all the comforts of a perfect hotel and in amazing surroundings, has to be high on the list of must-have holidays.

⇨ The above information is reprinted with kind permission from the International Tourism Trade Fairs Association (ITTFA). Visit www.ittfa.org for more information.

© International Tourism Trade Fairs Association

Sustainable tourism

Information from The World Bank.

Going around the world can be good for the world

Tourists. We've all made fun of them or been annoyed by them at some point or other; they snap photos incessantly, walk around with their noses buried in maps and crowd up our favourite hangouts. Well, here's something to keep in mind the next time you feel like wringing a tourist's neck: tourists happen to be important players in development. Here are a few examples of how tourism benefits people and economies.

Employment

One of the primary paths out of poverty is through employment, and tourism provides both direct and indirect employment through domestic industries like construction, agriculture, handicrafts, transport, food processing, manufacturing, fishing, services, retail, furniture-making, restaurants and bars, and accommodation.

Infrastructure

Increased tourism in an area usually means better roads, water and transportation systems as well as electricity and telecom services.

Cultural preservation

A country's historical sites, natural beauty, food and festivals can be big tourist attractions, so there is an incentive for governments to preserve and promote their country's culture.

Environmental preservation

Tourism can help preserve land for nature, and for many private and state-owned national parks tourism is the most important, if not the only, income generator. Tourism may also be among the only land-use options for income generation in ecologically fragile areas where many of the world's poorest people live. And when it comes to using the physical environment and biodiversity as income-generating assets, tourism is a less damaging option.

Economic benefits

Here are some facts about tourism's role in the economy:

⇨ Tourism contributes more than 10% of global GDP, and one in 12 jobs worldwide.

⇨ Tourism increases a country's foreign exchange earnings – tourists spend more than $200 billion annually in emerging market nations.

⇨ 46% of the workforce in tourism are women.

⇨ In 2008, international tourism generated $946 billion in export earnings.

⇨ Over the past six decades, tourism has expanded to become one of the largest and fastest-growing economic sectors in the world. Many new destinations have emerged alongside the traditional ones of Western Europe and North America. In fact, growth has been especially high in the world's emerging regions, and the share in international tourist arrivals received by developing countries has steadily risen, from 31% in 1990 to 45% in 2008.

THE WORLD BANK

⇨ The World Tourism Organization (UNWTO) predicts a growth in international tourist arrivals of between 3% and 4% in 2010.

Sources: Convention on Biological Diversity and World Tourism Organization

The dark side of tourism

Many of the above benefits of tourism have flip sides to them, i.e. when not managed right, tourism can cause more harm than good. And managing it right is exceptionally tricky; it requires government and private sector cooperation; tourism is so interlocked with society and the economy that there are too many stakeholders. This makes it a very complicated sector to manage.

Environmental

One of the most obvious concerns with tourism today is its impact on climate change, through the carbon footprint it leaves in air travel. The Ecumenical Coalition on Tourism estimates that tourism's share in global warming is up to 12.5%. According to a report of theirs, 'the global tourism industry is a significant contributor to climate change. Alarmingly, it is forecast that carbon emissions from tourism will grow by 162% in the period 2005–2035'. (While tourism is expected to boost climate change, for its part climate change is expected to hurt tourism. Changes in climate and weather patterns may affect tourists' comfort and travel plans. According to the UNWTO, 'changing demand patterns and tourist flows will have impacts on tourism businesses and on host communities, as well as "knock on" effects on related sectors, such as agriculture, handicrafts or construction.')

Other typical environmental problems associated with increased tourism are pollution and litter, as well as overcrowding and heavy traffic.

Socio-economic problems

⇨ When a place becomes a tourist hotspot, it often becomes too expensive for the locals.

⇨ Local culture sometimes gets lost in the quest for catering to tourist entertainment. In some cases, it has been observed that local street children do not even speak their own language; rather they speak languages from those countries whose citizens tend to visit their area the most.

⇨ Unskilled workers flocking to the area in search of jobs are often exploited and underpaid.

⇨ Tourism is great for entrepreneurship (encouraging lots of informal businesses), but it can also, unfortunately, encourage shadier entrepreneurship like drug-dealing and prostitution.

The Indonesian island of Bali, and Cancun in Mexico, are two places that have faced many of the above problems because of the breakneck speed at which tourism expanded there.

Making it sustainable

There are four pillars of sustainable tourism:

⇨ Effective sustainability planning.

⇨ Maximising social and economic benefits to the local community.

⇨ Reducing negative impacts to cultural heritage.

⇨ Reducing negative impacts to environmental heritage.

The International Finance Corporation (IFC), which is part of The World Bank Group, has a long history of investing in tourism in almost every country in the world, including some of the world's poorest countries. These projects mainly involve building hotels and tourist resorts, and ensuring sustainability – environmental, financial and social – is a fundamental part of the process. This includes ensuring things like training for employees, wastewater treatment, energy efficiency, water conservation, fire safety, and overall, ensuring that the project is financially sustainable and will be able to stand on its own feet.

Biodiversity and tourism

2010 is the International Year of Biodiversity. So, it's only fitting to take a look at the important crossover between biodiversity and tourism. And no, we're not talking about walruses with wanderlust or anything of the kind. The crossover between the two refers to the fact that many tourist activities depend on biodiversity. For example, people often travel to places to see the local wildlife, or they go hiking through tropical jungles, scuba diving, kayaking, etc.

So, that's an important reason for governments and policymakers to make sure biodiversity is protected: it is an important asset to the tourism industry. Here are some great examples from the Convention on Biological Diversity:

⇨ Wildlife conservancies in Namibia cover 11.9 million hectares of that country's world-renowned wildlife-rich plains. The conservancies have benefited more than 230,000 people in the form of jobs, cash dividends, game meat, skill building, and various social development projects. They have also permitted the recovery of various wildlife species including elephant, zebra, oryx, kudu and springbok.

⇨ Local tour guides in Tortuguero National Park, Costa Rica, earn two to four times the minimum wage in a five-month period. 359 ecotourism-related jobs have been created, and a local high school, clinic, and improved water and waste treatment facility have been established.

⇨ Between 2003 and 2005, tourism in four protected areas in New Zealand generated 4,000 jobs (the equivalent of 15% of all jobs in the four areas), NZ$130 million in direct household income, and NZ$560 million of revenue.

⇨ A sea turtle conservation initiative implemented in two communities in Brazil and Mexico, besides protecting the remaining sea turtle population in the two communities, has significantly improved local household welfare: family incomes, the percentage of homes with piped water, sewage and electricity, and the number of schools and clinics in each community had all increased since the beginning of the initiatives. Food and nutritional intake had also increased, as had the value of land in both areas.

Ecotourism can therefore be a great livelihood option for rural communities, but it's important that such projects be well planned. Poorly-planned and unregulated tourism development can greatly harm biodiversity, for example through unsustainable consumption of energy and fresh water, pollution, over-harvesting of local plant and animal biodiversity, and the unsustainable use of ecosystems such as coral reefs and forests. Also, infrastructure growth can destroy natural habitats. All of this in the long-run undermines the communities' ability to generate income through ecotourism.

What can you do?

If you're travelling somewhere, be aware of ways you can contribute to the local economy. For example, buying crafts from a roadside vendor will help someone's livelihood as opposed to buying something from the Duty Free store on your way out at the airport. Also, make sure you are always respectful of local cultures, and do not do anything to harm the environment.

Wherever you live, you can also help tourism in your country by supporting and learning about your cultural heritage and natural science in your area. Do your best to preserve the local environment and patronise locally-produced products and community-owned enterprises.

1 April 2010

⇨ The above information is reprinted with kind permission from The World Bank. To view the original source please visit http://youthink.worldbank.org/issues/environment/sustainable-tourism

Case study – the Maldives: lost in paradise

Information from Global Footprints.

The Maldives is perceived as the 'original paradise' for holidaymakers. But behind this image, nearly half of all Maldivians are living in poverty. The Maldives are seen as idyllic and close to perfection, the holiday destination of a lifetime: beautiful sandy beaches, turquoise sea and private resort islands. But on the flip side, many Maldivians have a very different experience. Tourism is the major industry in the Maldives, with the potential to stop poverty and improve local living conditions. But this is not happening... nearly half of the local population are living on just over $1 a day, which according to international standards means they are living in poverty. Maldivian people are suffering – fresh fruit and vegetables go directly to tourist islands, bypassing local people. The UN recently found over 30% of Maldivian children under five suffering from malnutrition, a situation as acute as Sub-Saharan Africa. Local people are unable to speak out about these awful conditions. The Government continues to impose severe restrictions on freedom of expression. Unfair trial, torture and imprisonment occur all too often.

⇨ The above information is reprinted with kind permission from Global Footprints. Visit www.globalfootprints.org for more information.

What is ecotourism?

Information from i-to-i.

The concept of ecotourism is one of ambiguity and dispute. There is no universal definition for ecotourism, nor is there a certifying agency. A common misconception is that ecotourism is just nature-based tourism, the act of surrounding yourself with nature's little wonders. The truth is far more complex. Ecotourism has to be both ecologically and socially conscious. Its goal is to minimise the impact that tourism has on an area through cooperation and management and in some cases it even encourages travellers to have a positive impact on their new surroundings.

A commonly accepted definition of ecotourism is:

'Responsible travel to natural areas that conserves the environment and improves the wellbeing of local people.'[1]

Ideally, ecotourism should...

⇨ Minimise the negative impacts of tourism;

⇨ Contribute to conservation efforts;

⇨ Employ locally and give money back to the community;

⇨ Educate visitors about the local environment and culture;

⇨ Cooperate with local people to manage natural areas;

⇨ Provide a positive experience for both visitor and host.

Eco-lodges

A hotel that is truly an 'eco-lodge' is one that makes efforts to conserve resources and limit waste. Some things a hotel can do to limit its environmental impact are:

⇨ Reducing temperatures for laundry water;

⇨ Changing sheets and towels less frequently;

⇨ Using solar power or alternative energy sources;

⇨ Installing low-flow showerheads and toilets;

⇨ Buying recycled products and recycling waste;

⇨ Building a compost heap or a waste-treatment facility.

Many hotels are keen to conserve energy because it both makes them look good and saves them a lot of money. Hotels that are sustainable also contribute to the local community. They buy local food products and hire local employees.

Greenwashing

With ecotourism being so popular, it is inevitable that many companies will claim to be environmentally friendly to get business. This is called 'greenwashing'. Since there is no single certifying agency to determine who actually engages in ecotourism, it is easy to get away with just throwing the term around.

> *A common misconception is that ecotourism is just nature-based tourism, the act of surrounding yourself with nature's little wonders. The truth is far more complex*

Many hotels claim to be eco-lodges simply because they have a good view. Wildlife-viewing trips are often labelled eco-tours even if they give nothing back to local ecology and sometimes cause significant problems to the area's wildlife. Just because something is in nature doesn't make it ecotourism. It's important to look more carefully at their practices to see if it really is ecotourism.

Homestays

A popular alternative to eco-lodges, especially for those who are travelling with a volunteer travel provider such as i-to-i, is to stay in homestay accommodation. The main benefit of this is that your accommodation costs will be going straight back into the community. In many cases your meals are also included and this usually means that local suppliers will benefit from your stay too.

Sustainable, alternative, responsible tourism – what does it all mean?

There are many other words to describe a similar idea. The terms 'ecotourism', 'sustainable tourism' or 'responsible tourism' are often used interchangeably. The main ideas behind these are all similar, but there are small differences.

Alternative tourism is any type of travel that is not mass tourism (i.e. beach vacations or traditional sightseeing tours). This includes ecotourism, backpacking, volunteer tourism, adventure tourism, historical tourism, tornado chasing, couch surfing or any other form of travel that is atypical.

The widely-accepted definition for sustainable tourism is 'Tourism that meets the needs of present tourists and host regions while protecting and enhancing opportunities

I-TO-I

for the future.'[1] It has the same ideals as ecotourism but is not limited to natural areas.

Responsible travel is a practice used by travellers guiding how they act in a host country. It has roots in sustainable tourism but focuses on being respectful as a guest in a foreign country, such as asking permission to take photographs or enter a home, observing some of the customs, such as dress, or making an effort to learn the language.

Note

1   The International Ecotourism Society (TIES)

⇨ The above information is reprinted with kind permission from i-to-i. Visit the i-to-i website at www.i-to-i.com for more information on this and other related topics.

© i-to-i

Coastal development problems: tourism

Each year a large percentage of holidaymakers head to coastlines around the world, where they have an enormous impact on marine ecosystems.

Massive influxes of tourists, often to a relatively small area, have a huge impact. They add to the pollution, waste and water needs of the local population, putting local infrastructure and habitats under enormous pressure. For example, 85% of the 1.8 million people who visit Australia's Great Barrier Reef are concentrated in two small areas, Cairns and the Whitsunday Islands, which together have a human population of just 130,000 or so.

Tourist infrastructure

In many areas, massive new tourist developments have been built – including airports, marinas, resorts and golf courses. Over-development for tourism has the same problems as other coastal developments, but often has a greater impact as the tourist developments are located at or near fragile marine ecosystems. For example:

⇨ mangrove forests and seagrass meadows have been removed to create open beaches;

⇨ tourist developments such as piers and other structures have been built directly on top of coral reefs;

⇨ nesting sites for endangered marine turtles have been destroyed and disturbed by large numbers of tourists on the beaches.

Careless resorts, operators and tourists

The damage doesn't end with the construction of tourist facilities.

Some resorts empty their sewage and other wastes directly into water surrounding coral reefs and other sensitive marine habitats.

Recreational activities also have a huge impact. For example, careless boating, diving, snorkelling and fishing have substantially damaged coral reefs in many parts of the world, through people touching reefs, stirring up sediment, and dropping anchors.

Marine animals such as whale sharks, seals, dugongs, dolphins, whales and birds are also disturbed by increased numbers of boats, and by people approaching too closely.

Tourism can also add to the consumption of seafood in an area, putting pressure on local fish populations and sometimes contributing to over-fishing.

Some resorts empty their sewage and other wastes directly into water surrounding coral reefs

---

Collection of corals, shells and other marine souvenirs – either by individual tourists, or local people who then sell the souvenirs to tourists – also has a detrimental effect on the local environment.

Floating towns

The increased popularity of cruise ships has also adversely affected the marine environment. Carrying up to 4,000 passengers and crew, these enormous floating towns are a major source of marine pollution through the dumping of rubbish and untreated sewage at sea, and the release of other shipping-related pollutants.

⇨ The above information is reprinted with kind permission from WWF Global. Visit wwf.panda.org for more information.

© WWF (panda.org). Some rights reserved.

I-TO-I / WWF

Can wildlife tourism help conserve our endangered species?

Wildlife-watching holidays often focus on the iconic species such as whales, tigers and polar bears, many of which are often the most threatened. So can wildlife tourism help conserve our endangered species?

By Holly Foat

Some people believe these endangered animals should be kept away from tourists, wrapped up in cotton wool, and some even believe that they should be taken out of the wild to be kept in captivity as a 'reserve' to prevent extinction. However, this is preservation rather than conservation and is treating the symptoms, not finding a cure. Conservation is about more than saving animals; conservation is maintaining habitats and changing opinions. Animals are primarily endangered by the actions of people, from deforestation to pollution and hunting. Wildlife tourism can have a role to play in stopping detrimental activities by increasing awareness and encouraging people to relish rather than ravish the natural environment.

Tiger holidays

No trip to India is complete without a trip to one of the tiger reserves to see the majestic tiger in its native habitat. Unfortunately, poaching of tigers still continues, not only for bones for Chinese medicine but for skins for fashion in Tibet and China. The only way to protect tigers is through official legislation and better policing which many charities lobby for. But through well-managed tiger tourism, the countries that are home to these beautiful animals can benefit from the financial income brought into their economy and realise that protecting tigers isn't just good for their image but also good for their pockets. Increasing numbers of tourists will also raise awareness of the plight of the tiger and help increase publicity for the campaigners.

Whale watching

Whale watching is a rapidly growing industry and is incredibly widespread with major whale-watching operations all over the world. Sadly, as most whales aren't endangered species, whaling (albeit under the guise of scientific purposes) is still carried out in Japan, Norway and Iceland. Recently, Japan has called to resume commercial whaling. In response to the continued whaling, conservation organisations have appealed for signatures to petition the governments of these countries until they cease whaling. Another option to oppose whaling is to support the whale-watching industry in the countries that continue to catch whales so that the authorities realise that the increasing revenue brought in by whale watching is a far more reliable and sustainable addition to the economy than whaling.

Dolphin watching

Dolphin tourism is a growing industry and many areas have already felt the financial benefits brought in by increasing tourist numbers. Most locations in the West have now set up codes of conduct to protect dolphins. However, dolphins are still at risk in many areas where tourism hasn't yet taken off. With the sad loss of the baji (Yangtze river dolphin) fresh in our minds it seems clear that if China had an established dolphin-watching industry things could be very different today. The conservational value of wildlife tourism has already been recognised in the Amazon where river dolphin tourism has already started and will hopefully save these river dolphins from the same fate.

> **Conservation is about more than saving animals; conservation is maintaining habitats and changing opinions**

Wildlife tourism can be instrumental in raising awareness and changing attitudes towards animals. By making each individual animal more valuable alive than dead, it can be possible to encourage both poachers and governments to refrain from killing and to seek out alternative ways to profit from them. Rather than trying to enforce conservation efforts at an international level, the use of tourism to change views at a local level is far more powerful. By viewing animals as a valuable commodity and a key component in the tourism industry, rather than a pest or foodstuff, it is more likely that conservation initiatives will be implemented and successful, ensuring that future generations can visit, watch and enjoy these wonderful creatures.

⇨ The above information is reprinted with kind permission from Responsibletravel.com. Visit www.responsibletravel.com for more information.

© Responsible travel.com

'Green people' in global tourism – a new way to travel

Who doesn't like a good vacation? A great vacation can be a lazy beach holiday relaxing with a cocktail or getting lost hiking in the mountains among spectacular views. Unfortunately, most vacations we enjoy cause nature a lot of stress.

By Ksenya Kopilovsky

A report by the United Nations Environmental Programme (UNEP, 2003) on the subject of tourism and biodiversity suggests that 'resource depletion and habitat disruption, littering and water pollution are problems associated with mainstream tourism that can have negative consequences for biodiversity conservation'. But in the late 1980s, people found a new way of exploring the Earth's wonders and it has been evolving and becoming more popular ever since.

According to the World Travel & Tourism Council, tourism generates nearly 11% of Global Domestic Product (GDP), making it one of the largest industries on the planet (if not the largest). Nearly 700 million people travel outside of their countries for various purposes (vacation, business, medical) every year, many making their way to resorts in the global 'hot spots', such as the Caribbean Islands, Ocean Islands, the Cape Floristic Region of South Africa, the Mediterranean and New Zealand.

The global footprint of mass tourism on the ecosystems is anything but positive and because most tourism development is driven by the private sector, the local communities mostly don't benefit from the natural attractions on their lands or waters (or don't benefit from a fair share). However, tourism also harbours a great potential to benefit economies and conservation if only managed fairly and undertaken responsibly.

Ecotourism can be 'passive' – buying your holiday package from companies that donate part of their proceedings to local charities, booking environmentally-friendly accommodation and searching for ethical guarantees on the holiday provider's brochure or website.

> **The global footprint of mass tourism on the ecosystems is anything but positive and because most tourism development is driven by the private sector, the local communities mostly don't benefit**

'Active ecotourism is a way for people to enjoy all that nature has to offer and leave a positive mark on the environment,' says Jonathan Gilben, the founder of Go-Eco, an international VolunTourism organisation. His organisation is just one of many similar holiday providers offering people the chance to experience nature a little differently. The International Ecotourism Society asserts that demand for this type of holidaymaking 'is growing at ten to 12% per annum in the international market.'

Voluntourists are tourists with a 'twist': they prefer to experience a new place not by sitting in a tourist bus and listening to a pre-recorded guide, but by physically connecting with the place and its inhabitants, whether they be humans or animals. Their approach to holidaymaking makes a world of difference and greatly benefits the places and communities they choose to visit. Guided and supported by the various organisations' instructors, voluntourists have helped local communities to plant hundreds of trees in the Amazon rainforests in Costa Rica, care and rehabilitate abandoned or orphaned animals at Drakensberg escarpment in the Limpopo Province of South Africa and helped remote communities in Iceland to conserve the Þingvellir Park (a UNESCO World Heritage Site).

The financial input (which varies depending on the organisation, the length of the trip and the destination) is of paramount importance to the host communities. The International Ecotourism Society lists tourism as the principal export of 83% of developing countries and prime export of 33% of the poorest countries.

On the other hand, mass-tourism expenses for all-inclusive packages hardly ever reach the natives, since they pay for airlines, hotels, guides and other international companies. Without the help of charity or non-profit voluntour organisations, developing countries, which are the most popular destinations for voluntourism, would not have been able to fund such programmes themselves. Of the minimum fee the organisations charge from the voluntourists, only a small part (12%, according to Global Aware) is spent on administration, while the rest covers meals, accommodation, on-site travel, donations to the various community projects, orientation packages, medical emergency evacuation and medical insurance.

Biodiversity is, arguably, the biggest beneficiary as coincidently most of the biodiversity 'hot spots' are located in the world's developing and poor countries. Even if the projects do not involve preservation per se, they help local people construct and repair means that will help them in nature conservation, such as installation of identifying signs in rainforests (Costa Rica), helping with sustainable food production (Cuba), cleaning up local rivers (Jamaica) and building ecologically sustainable reforested habitats (Thailand). Some of the

voluntours that do focus on biodiversity conservation allow for some 'nature freaks' to realise lifelong dreams and assist in caring for endangered animals, like the Giant Panda project in Japan (Go-Eco) or the Animal Sanctuary project in Ecuador (Green Force) where voluntourists not only interact with wildlife and help maintain its wellbeing, but also educate the locals about the need to protect wildlife and monitor and expose bad practice towards animals.

Mass-tourism expenses for all-inclusive packages hardly ever reach the natives since they pay for airlines, hotels, guides and other international companies

The variety of destinations, activities and costs make ecotourism, and particularly voluntourism, attractive to more and more holidaymakers around the world. The International Ecotourism Society reports a 34% annual growth in demand for ecotours in the past 20 years and sector analysts predict more growth, suggesting that 'early converts to sustainable tourism will make market gains'. No special skills are required to become an ecotourist, only a taste for adventure, fun and a pinch of selflessness.

12 August 2011

⇨ The above information is reprinted with kind permission from Earth Times. Visit www.earthtimes.org for more information.

© Earth Times

How your travels will affect local communities

With concern for the environment growing rapidly and increasing pressure being placed on travellers to travel responsibly, it's hardly surprising that the ecotourism industry is booming. But even within the realm of ecotourism, the social implications of travel are often overlooked.

Negative impacts

Tourism can have a negative impact on local communities when carried out without respect or consideration. Indeed, tourism can cause hostility, competition, jealousy and the loss or destruction of the local culture. Many travellers fail to research before they go and simple mistakes which can often be avoided are often made, causing offence to local people and making the lives of the next travellers to visit that little bit more difficult. It's vitally important that you make an effort to fit in, to limit the impact of your presence and to show your respect for the traditions and culture of the community that you are staying in. Otherwise, you are likely to confirm the bad reputation that travellers are gradually developing.

Loss of culture

Loss of culture can take many forms. One major change can be seen in the production of souvenirs. Once tourists arrive in an area, the local people realise that money can be made by selling their crafts to visitors. After a while, though, crafts which once had a spiritual or cultural significance suddenly are just goods. Some designs may be changed to meet tourists' demands and lose all cultural value.

Tourism can have a negative impact on local communities when carried out without respect or consideration

Tourists are often unwilling to completely immerse themselves in the local culture and this means that in order to keep your custom, local communities must adjust to your needs. Traditional food, wares and customs are replaced with those of the traveller's homeland, effectively creating a home away from home. Yet by doing this, by demanding that destinations change to meet your demand you are taking away the very essence of travel. Therefore, in order to travel responsibly you must accept your surroundings for what they are and not expect anything else.

Culture clashes

Tourists are frequently disrespectful of local customs. Women (and men) often walk around in revealing clothing when the social norm is to politely cover yourself up. This is particularly important in places of worship and it is often considered extremely rude. This behaviour can cause ill will and can also cause the local people to stray from their beliefs and customs.

Ill will can also be caused by the way tourists interact with locals. Many take pictures of local people like animals in the zoo, without subtlety or permission, then move on without purchasing any of their crafts.

Physical influences

Tourism can lead to overuse of natural resources, vandalism and crime. Competition for local resources is a huge problem in tourist areas. Resorts use an enormous amount of water to run a golf course, depriving local people of drinking water. Similarly, grazing land may be destroyed for resort development, thereby significantly damaging the ability of local communities to maintain their traditional lifestyles.

Frequently local people are denied access to areas that have been set up as tourist destinations. Local people can no longer play on nearby beaches or visit the local national park, which doesn't give them much incentive to protect it. This is more often an indirect consequence of tourism as local people simply cannot afford the prices that tourists can.

Positive impacts

Before you get too depressed by the negative impacts of tourism, remember that with a little consideration, much of the problem can be solved. If you travel respectfully there is no reason why you can't minimise these impacts. In fact, tourism can have positive impacts on the culture as well. Making an effort to meet local people will give you a more accurate insight into the way they live their lives and make the interaction more pleasurable for both parties.

1-TO-1

Reduce stereotypes

When people from different backgrounds get the chance to connect, they have the opportunity to see each other as individuals and not the nationalities they represent. Travel is a wonderful opportunity to talk to people and let them see that you, as an individual, do not fit into all the negative stereotypes of your ethnicity. And likewise, not all indigenous people are what you expect them to be. Making an effort to meet people can reduce these negative perceptions and stereotypes and develop appreciation and understanding of different cultures. People who live in developing countries are often extremely friendly and if you show them a little respect they will be able to introduce you to a side of your destination that you never knew existed.

Develop facilities

As long as the welfare of the local community isn't disregarded, creating facilities for tourism can benefit the local population as well. Tourism development brings money to the region and also forces improvement of local facilities like roads and water supplies. These two things together can easily help to develop the infrastructure of an area. Tourism can create new recreational or entertainment facilities, health systems, restaurants or public spaces. The longer tourism thrives in the area, the more improvements will be made.

Strengthen communities

If the money being made in a community is staying there, it can decrease emigration from the area. It can pay for a new school or community centre. It can bring the community together to create tourist facilities such as a local restaurant or visitors' centre. They can also work together to manage tourism in the area and the profits will go directly to the community.

Create pride

When tourists come to see an authentic ceremony, the local people realise that they are unique. They take pride in the fact that people are interested in them. They take pride in their natural surroundings, heritage and art. Tourism can cause indigenous people to revive old traditions and preserve customs that may otherwise soon be lost to globalisation.

Create jobs

A true eco-tourism organisation employs local people. If people from the community have jobs in the tourism industry this will improve their economic situation and also decrease hard feelings towards tourists.

If organisations work with the local community and hire local residents it opens employment opportunities up to people to whom opportunities are rarely available. It offers them the motivation to learn and to develop their skills and gives them the opportunity to build a better life for themselves. The bottom line is, it gives them hope.

Local people make perfect guides. They know the area they live in. They may know more about the plants in their back yard than a university-educated botanist would. They can imitate birdcalls and track animals. Hiring local guides is not only better for the community, it's better for the visitor too.

There is a fine line between tourism and responsible tourism. At first a community is keen on bringing tourists into the area. They see it as easy money. But bringing too many tourists into a place causes animosity and loss of culture. Sometimes it's difficult to see the damage that is being done to a community until it is too late, even if you're an active member of that community. The key to the development of sustainable tourism is effective management. It's up to you to be sensitive to cultures other than your own and make the effort to travel with companies that truly are eco-friendly, but it is also up to local governments and communities to ensure that they are controlling tourism and monitoring its effects on both local communities and environments.

⇨ The above information is reprinted with kind permission from i-to-i. Visit www.i-to-i.com for more information.

Integrating ethics into tourism: beyond codes of conduct

The industry is faced with increasingly pressing challenges but embedding ethics into core strategy makes good business sense.

As the world's largest service industry, contributing an estimated 5% to worldwide GDP, tourism creates both jobs and wealth but also has clear social and environmental consequences. The industry is therefore faced with a range of increasingly pressing challenges.

Over the last few years, hotel companies have made a determined effort to deal with the impact their business activities have on the environment, particularly by measuring and reducing their carbon and water footprints. Both major international hospitality companies and small businesses recognise that there are tangible benefits in doing this, including real efficiency gains and an improved corporate reputation.

Another closely-linked challenge for companies is how to manage the ethical operation of their business. Ethical issues arise in four main areas: the supply chain, the local community (in the tourism destination), the workplace, and customers. There may be concerns about forced labour in the supply chain or exploitation of migrant workers in the workplace, for example; or local people may – often rightly – perceive that they have little or no share in the economic benefits of tourism, while bearing a disproportionate burden from environmental degradation.

Ethical issues arise in four main areas: the supply chain, the local community (in the tourism destination), the workplace, and customers

In 1999, the UN World Tourism Organization (UNWTO) devised and adopted a global code of ethics for tourism, designed to minimise the negative effects of tourism activity on destinations and local communities, which was officially recognised by the UN in 2001. Now, the UNWTO is holding the first International Congress on Ethics and Tourism (15-16 September 2011, Madrid), arguably the first opportunity to evaluate whether the industry has moved beyond symbolic statements and agreed codes to concrete actions.

Encouragingly, there is evidence that the hotel industry is assuming a proactive, collective approach to human rights and business ethics, incorporating human rights risk mapping, employee training on responsible business, and sustainable local benefits. Major hotel companies have taken significant steps in the past decade to integrate policies on human rights into their stated policies on business conduct and ethics.

How in practice can the global hospitality industry advance ethical and socially-responsible tourism? One concrete initiative is the Youth Career Initiative supported by several major international hotel companies. This six-month education programme gives disadvantaged young people aged 18 to 21 hands-on experience and training in an international hotel. Apart from gaining life and work skills, young participants are empowered to make informed career choices, enabling them to improve their employability and enhance their long-term social and economic opportunities.

Over 420 young people in 11 countries participate in the programme every year in more than 50 leading hotels. The high number (85%) of young people graduating from this scheme to secure employment in the hotel industry or in further education shows that this project effectively tackles key issues of youth unemployment and social exclusion, poverty, and exploitation. In addition, a pilot programme to rehabilitate survivors of human trafficking will be run soon in hotels in Mexico, Brazil and Vietnam.

Among specific initiatives, Marriott International relaunched their business ethics awareness programme last year, which provides employees with the tools to identify potential ethical and compliance issues and raise them with the appropriate leaders within the organisation. This includes a new training video for all new hire inductions, plus quarterly bulletins with updates on tools for prevention. The company recently developed human rights and protection of children training for their security officers and all property-based employees, which is being rolled out across their global operations.

Another company with a proactive ethical policy is Shangri-La Hotels and Resorts, a Hong Kong-based hotel group operating globally but with half of its properties in China. They launched a supplier code of conduct in 2009 (now externally audited) and conduct site visits to their top 150 suppliers to check employee wages and conditions, health and safety, management

THE GUARDIAN

systems and environmental practices; they have a group-wide programme linking hotels with a local school or orphanage for five to ten years, including providing training in hotel skills.

The examples highlighted still represent best practice rather than industry-wide reality. There is much more to be done. A code of ethics and human rights policy is no longer enough: companies need to show practical examples of where they have made a difference through the supply chain, local communities, their workplace, and to their customers' behaviour. Embedding ethics into core business strategy makes good business sense as it potentially enhances a company's profits, management effectiveness, public image and employee relations.

Hospitality companies that do take a long-term view, and marry high ethical standards with practical measures, are likely to prove the winners in a fast-changing industry. The Madrid UNWTO conference should provide an interesting snapshot of whether the industry has really grasped the nature of this challenge.

© Guardian News and Media Limited 2011

Amazon town bans tourists

Nazareth in Colombia says travellers don't spend much and show little respect to indigenous people.

By Toby Muse

The small Amazonian town of Nazareth is a traveller's dream. Wildlife prowls the surrounding jungles and indigenous inhabitants practise ceremonies that long predate the arrival of the Spanish *conquistadores*.

But it may be advisable for tourists to give the place a wide berth. Locals have declared their town off-limits to travellers, even though this stretch of the Amazon river is playing host to more visitors than ever. Their main complaint: tourists' behaviour, and that only a fraction of the money they spend trickles down to the indigenous. 'What we earn here is very little. Tourists come here, they buy a few things, a few artisan goods, and they go. It is the travel agencies that make the good money,' said Juvencio Pereira, an Indigenous Guard, Nazareth's unofficial volunteer police force.

The town of 800 people, a 20-minute boat ride from the tourist hub of Leticia, takes its ban seriously. At the entrance, Pereira and other guards stand armed with their traditional sticks to deter unwelcome visitors. Nazareth resident Grimaldo Ramos feels that some tourists can't distinguish between the wildlife and the Amazon's residents, snapping photos of indigenous families as if they were another animal. 'Tourists come and shove a camera in our faces,' he said. 'Imagine if you were sitting in your home and strangers came in and started taking photos of you. You wouldn't like it.'

Nazareth's actions reveal a split among the indigenous communities that live along the river about what role tourism should play in the region's development.

With the rise of eco-tourism, this part of the Amazon, which joins Colombia, Peru and Brazil, has seen a flood of travellers arriving to experience the world's most biologically diverse region. Tourists swim with the Amazon's pink dolphins, fish for piranhas, hike through the rainforests and take in the sunsets over the mighty river. According to the tourism office for the Colombian province of Amazonas, the 35,000 people who trekked to the region in 2010 represent a fivefold surge in numbers over the past eight years. But as Nazareth complains, the indigenous people have so far seen little of the benefits, mostly just the sharp end of tourism.

A common concern among indigenous leaders is that local children are adopting the outsiders' ways, with many children more comfortable in 'western' dress and listening to the imported music of reggaeton and Colombia's vallenato. There are misunderstandings of two cultures interacting. What a tourist may consider polite curiosity about indigenous culture can seem to some here intrusive and even an attempt to gain sacred tribal wisdom. 'We don't like it when they ask members of the community about our traditional knowledge and the medicines we possess,' said Pereira.

Other communities, however, take the view that the number of visitors to the region is going to rise, so they might as well profit from it. A couple of hours downriver lies Puerto Narino, whose mayor, Nelson Ruiz, understands Nazareth's worries, but says that if tourism is well-regulated it can help lift communities out of the poverty that troubles much of this zone.

He added that visitors are expected to abide by certain rules, such as no drug taking and no sexual tourism.

25 March 2011

© Guardian News and Media Limited 2011

Slumming it

The current generation crystallises the death of the package-holiday tourist and the birth of the post-modern 'traveller'. Holly Young questions the ethical, economic and educational value of poverty tourism.

It would come as a surprise should anyone reading this not know of someone with tales of 'slumming it'. Our generation crystallises the death of the package holiday tourist and the birth of the post-modern 'traveller': holidays are now 'travels' and escapism is rebranded as a search for meaning and enlightenment. Backpacker culture is not simply about travelling on a budget. It is, to a greater or lesser extent, about buying into this search for authenticity – for the 'real' India, for the 'typical' Bolivian village, for the most potent culture shock available. One of the most intriguing expressions of this Holy Grail has been the way in which sun, sea and sex has been traded in for squalor.

Is the irony that the slum tour market incentivises the preservation of poverty?

You would be right to argue that this is hardly new; that it is more of a 60s hangover than a contemporary cultural phenomenon. What is new, however, is the extent to which it is now accessible. This 'alternative' travelling experience has become mainstream tourism. Slum tours across the world from Rio de Janeiro to Cape Town to *Slumdog Millionaire*'s Dharavi slum in Mumbai have, since the mid-1990s, increasingly capitalised on this captive market. It becomes difficult, then, to distance oneself from the clichéd 'gap yah' figure: what has become the parody of the post-modern tourist. We are predisposed to see this tourist in terms of economic and cultural exploitation, of neo-colonial cultural condescension and faux philanthropy. It is this cultural backdrop that has fed the ferocity of the media backlash to which this kind of tourism has been subjected. It is seen, along with 'disaster tourism', as the more sinister corner of a wider bracket of poverty tourism that encompasses 'voluntourism' and cultural exchanges, spawning scathing terms such as 'poor voyeurism', 'poorism' and 'poverty porn'.

Critiques of the fetishisation of poverty have been accompanied by debates over the extent to which slum tours benefit development. The link between development and tourism is well established. Developing countries have for a long time acknowledged the opportunities of foreign exchange and the employment it affords. It has a substantial ability to contribute to GDP. It is not only luxury tourism but backpacking that is recognised in this capacity. Although generally speaking less profitable, the perceived asymmetry between meaningful experience and areas of economic growth enables backpacking to be a means of economically penetrating marginalised areas, both rural and poor. Developing countries, with their unexploited natural and cultural riches, readily cater for this market. Stimulation of foreign investment and social regeneration are the perceived outcomes of tourism as a poverty panacea. It is within this discourse that tours justify themselves. Both the Favela and Dharavi slum tours make a point of bringing you to the community schools that their profits fund – enabling immediate validation of the connection between your $34 fee and the global project of human development.

It would, however, be naive to accept this narrative without scepticism. Although there are credible organisations, such as Dharavi's Reality Tours and Travel, which are able to prove their not-for-profit status, altruistic market ventures inevitably attract those wishing to exploit. There is particular opportunity for false advertising in developing countries where there is often an absence of state economic regulation. Besides management issues such as benefit distribution and sensitivity to local residents, there is also scope for more substantive anxieties about the theory connecting poverty tourism to development. Is this merely a temporary makeshift solution to poverty? There is a genuine danger that communities will become too dependent on the industry. Is the irony that the slum tour market incentivises the preservation of poverty?

Slum tourism is not without its success stories. Tours in the villages of Mayange, one hour south of Kigali, Rwanda, are led by New Dawn Associates, a Rwandan social enterprise tourist agency, alongside Rwanda Nziza, a locally-run tourism cooperative which provides training in tourism for its members and shares the profits. Of the $60 per head that the tour costs, 70% of the revenue is given back to the community members that participate in the tour. To maintain equality of distribution, the community participants are on a rotation system. The scope for growth is shown by the example of local cooks being so successful that the tourism cooperative invested $10,000 in a restaurant for them. A demonstration of the way in which all this can be not only financially fruitful but socially empowering is found in the large weaving cooperative run by a group of women for whom increased sales brought greater

THE OXONIAN GLOBALIST

independence and wealth. It appears, then, that the link between tourism and development is not necessarily a fallacy. The key is in regulating the legitimacy of tour management.

While slum tours are not innately problematic, the ethical dimensions complicate the issue. Taking a step back from the charged discussions amongst the countless blogs and articles which slum tours have generated, it becomes clear the issue is not simply 'is it right to pay to look at a poor person?' but who attributes meaning to the experience. How are we led to understand the culture shock? The promotional literature of slum tourism claims to sell you insight and understanding, yet the media backlash argues that the experience entrenches ignorance. More than that, it deceives. Dharavi's Reality Tours and Travel demonstrates the trend in poverty representation of inverting the image of the glassy-eyed slum child with outstretched arms and replacing it with the neoliberal citizen, a slum-dweller smiling beside newly-made handicrafts. The subtext: not all poor people are lazy, and you are invited to admire the 'spirit' of the people. Yet some argue that this reduces development to the stimulation of entrepreneurship. Tourists leave with no understanding of the complexities of removing structural inequality. Indeed, as Reality Tours and Travel's website hints, there may be more pressing issues at stake: 'It is quite an adventure to pass through the narrow alleys, and you will almost certainly lose your sense of direction!'

While slum tours are not innately problematic, the ethical dimensions complicate the issue

The most critical omission of the tours has been their failure to situate the slum within the global context. The social and economic disfranchisement of slum dwellers is mirrored geographically by their confinement to particular urban areas. Subsequently slums have been conceptualised as legal black holes 'outside' the city. This has understandably attracted fascination but also, problematically, the portrayal of slums as 'exceptional' spaces. The *UN Habitat* report makes it clear that slums are far from exceptional. Rather, they are fast becoming the norm. Slums must be understood not as transient spaces in the trajectory of modernisation but expanding, structurally integral elements of neoliberal development. Mike Davies, in his influential essay *Planet of Slums*, described slums as warehouses for a surplus humanity. The Pentagon has anticipated that the growth in the gulf between the urban rich and the urban poor renders cities the natural battleground of the 21st century. These evaluations appear drastically at odds with the image of the slums as sites of progress, undermining the justification of slum tours' existence.

Furthermore, rather than being sites of cultural osmosis and understanding, boundaries are reconfirmed: slum tours transform tourists' reality into a zoo in which the slums' inhabitants are objectified and 'othered' in the act of reflexivity. It is a canvas not for transgression but for the confirmation of the superiority of Western values and understanding of development as economic growth. It is a simulation of the ethnographic experience made accessible to the masses. Tourists consume a staged reality and return home with the badge of 'authentic' travel.

While this discourse is seductive, it oozes self-righteousness. It is unsurprisingly produced in the main by those engaged in development projects. Implicit is the message that engaging in development should be left to the development elite, and is not for the participation of the masses. While the necessity of education in the issues of development is undeniable for those working towards it, the by-product of these critiques is a demonisation of the initiative to understand conditions of poverty. This is equally as problematic as the romanticisation of poverty. Reconceptualising this positive impulse as a distasteful cliché threatens to delegitimise the basis of global understanding and empathy. Perhaps a limited understanding of poverty is better than no understanding at all.

It is thus tempting for the sake of journalistic punch to regurgitate the sensationalist viewpoints flooding the web, but this would not move the debate forward. In this context, the sensible line is more controversial. What is needed is a more balanced narrative of slum tourism that filters out both the sensational and the misleading. Perhaps this is a convenient way of coming to terms with the fact that, despite finding the critiques convincing, I still could not deny my interest in visiting a slum. My conscience was eased upon discovering that slum tours can also be, given the right preconditions, beneficial for development. Furthermore, resignation to their existence is pragmatic; with such a fast-growing market they are not going anywhere any time soon. The critical pitfall is the confusion of the post-modern tourist's search for meaning with development itself. Education about the complexities of poverty mitigation is key in fostering consumer awareness so that the tours are seen for what they are: interesting but artificial. This will enable tourists to resist being sold the culture shock experience as anything more glorified or constructive than a personal revelation.

13 February 2011

⇨ The above information is reprinted with kind permission from *The Oxonian Globalist*. Visit www.toglobalist.org for more information on this and other related topics.

© *The Oxonian Globalist*

THE OXONIAN GLOBALIST

Responsible tourism

Information from the Foreign and Commonwealth Office.

You may hear many different phrases used for this topic...'Green tourism' is a term widely used to convey what we mean by responsible, ethical or sustainable tourism. All of these terms mean pretty much the same thing and are generally used to convey tourism that is good for the people and environment in holiday destinations.

Going on a green holiday doesn't mean that you have to stop visiting your favourite destination, nor does it mean camping in the wilderness without all of your luxuries! These are some common misconceptions that holidaymakers have, but in reality it is much more simple than everyone thinks.

Summing up responsible tourism

You can sum up responsible tourism in relation to three key areas:

⇨ PEOPLE: Local people should get a fair deal out of your visit, by offering goods or services for you to enjoy – such as great-tasting, authentic food from a local restaurant, real local crafts for you to take home as a lasting souvenir or guiding services so you can get closer to the destination that you're visiting.

⇨ PLACES: It's really important that holidays help conserve our precious natural environment and the amazing wildlife within it. Beautiful environments are what make holidays special! Greener travel ensures that any 'nature' excursion or tour is taken by guides who know how to preserve the natural environment and wildlife.

⇨ CLIMATE: This is about your carbon footprint. There are lots of simple ways for you to reduce your carbon emissions whilst on holiday – see our top tips below.

By making small changes in the way that we travel, we can all make a difference and ensure that the destinations we love to visit will be here for future generations to enjoy!

Follow our top ten green travel tips to become a responsible tourist:

1 Buy locally – buying locally-made souvenirs and eating and drinking at local cafés and restaurants are great ways to get into the holiday spirit, and also benefit the local community.

2 Respect the local culture and traditions – dress and act appropriately for the place that you are visiting. Do a little background reading before you go away or ask your holiday rep for advice.

3 Please use water sparingly – take short showers rather than baths, and inform staff if you are happy to reuse towels and bed linen rather than having them replaced daily. Many hot countries suffer from periods of drought and this will help to conserve water.

4 Please try to remove packaging from items that you are taking away with you – many countries are currently unable to cope with high levels of waste, and do not have recycling services as we do in the UK.

5 Get closer to the country you're visiting by booking excursions with local suppliers and tour guides – it will enrich your experience and help to support the local economy. If booking via your holiday company, ask your holiday rep, or at your hotel reception if the excursions use local suppliers. Hire a car only if you have to: it is much more environmentally friendly to use public transport, cycle or walk to explore the area you are visiting.

6 Turn down/off heating and air-conditioning when not required – and turn off the TV rather than leaving it on standby.

7 Please do not step on, touch or remove any coral – it is important to protect the coral reefs when snorkelling, they are extremely fragile.

8 In some parts of the world it is worth thinking twice about having your photo taken with 'wild animals' – there are some countries where animals are taken from the wild and exploited in this way when young, and may then be mistreated or killed when they get too large or difficult to handle.

9 Book safari trips with a licensed and trained guide – so that you can enjoy your day out and the wild animals are not disturbed or threatened by your presence.

10 Please don't buy products made from endangered or wild animals and plants – including coral, shells, starfish, horns, teeth, and animal skins and fur. Endangered plants and animals need our help to protect them!

⇨ The above information is reprinted with kind permission from the Foreign and Commonwealth Office. Visit www.fco.gov.uk for more information.

© Crown copyright 2011

Volunteer tourism defies recession but is this positive news for the South?

Information from the International Institute for Environment and Development.

By Kate Lee

Despite reports that the international tourism market has suffered during the downturn, one strand of tourism – the gap year and volunteer tourism market – seems to have flourished. This can partly be attributed to the increase in redundancies, which has prompted more people to take time out to reflect on what to do next and to gain a new perspective on life. Shortage of graduate jobs has also encouraged undergraduates to escape the gloomy outlook at home to gain valuable work experience and to give their CVs a winning edge for when they return. This influx of volunteers to the South, armed with the desire to contribute time, money and skills to a poorer society, is surely a good thing. Or is it?

Volunteering abroad is often seen as a win–win enterprise. Individuals gain enriching life experiences, get to travel to a different country and can add to their CV while making a difference to someone's life or protecting the environment. However, it is this notion that volunteering abroad can always 'make a difference' that is damaging. Volunteers are led to believe they have the appropriate skills and cultural understanding to meet the perceived needs of the developing world without stepping back to think about what exactly it is they are contributing and whether it is of use.

The projects that volunteer tourism organisations promote encourage volunteers to think that development is something that can be 'done' to the poor – teaching, building, caring. Whilst all these activities are not in themselves inherently bad, they encourage a simplistic view of development, and reinforce power relations in favour of the developed world; poor people have needs that volunteers can understand and meet whilst those in the developing world cannot.

Profits before ethics?

The voluntary tourism sector is now largely driven by the market and the demands of tourists, so host communities have little power over how things are developed, managed and run. They rarely have a say in what happens where and why. A report by Tourism Concern highlighted that many volunteer organisations do not even ask for feedback from the project host.

There are currently few mechanisms in place to monitor and evaluate projects. Because volunteer tourism is predominately a profit-driven sector, few programmes have skill-set requirements or formal contracts for volunteers; the only requirement is their money (of which little actually ends up with the project either). The value of a volunteer with no relevant experience or useful skills, who stays for a short period of time and has limited understanding of the local culture or language, is highly questionable. Voluntary Service Overseas (VSO) also highlighted this back in 2007, as the gap year market really began to expand.

Reinforcing or reducing inequality and difference?

The nature of volunteer tourism (being demand driven) is such that the pattern of volunteering does not necessarily reflect real need or poverty levels. Many of the most vulnerable countries are regarded as unsafe and therefore may be undesirable to volunteers. Far more attractive is somewhere exotic, safe, warm and offering a degree of adventure and interaction with different cultures or charismatic animals. In the majority of cases volunteer tourism is first and foremost a holiday.

The voluntary tourism sector is now largely driven by the market... so host communities have little power over how things are developed

Volunteering often reduces the world to the developed and the developing – reinforcing differences between the 'poor' and the 'rich' rather than promoting similarities and encouraging the exchange of ideas. Differences are emphasised through a lack of understanding of the complex issues surrounding people's needs. For example, volunteers can come into close contact with poverty. But instead of critically questioning and engaging with issues, poverty is rationalised as something that happens to the poor.

Worse still, volunteers often come away reasoning that people are poor but happy. Poverty is not viewed as something that can be experienced by people anywhere, but as something suffered by people in the developing world. How often have we heard someone say: 'Volunteering abroad made me feel so lucky and learn to appreciate what I have'? The systems and structures at the heart of the problem are never called into question.

Many of the most vulnerable countries are regarded as unsafe and therefore may be undesirable to volunteers

Here to stay?

Volunteer tourism is not going to disappear. In order for the sector to bring benefits to hosts as well as tourists it needs to be driven at a local level to meet local needs. Yet, at the same time, the industry must be better aligned at a global level in order to maximise opportunities and support. Regulations must be put in place for companies that send volunteers abroad – to ensure greater transparency about where money goes and how involved host communities are in planning and managing projects, and with local investment into projects and long-term commitment from the volunteer organisation. But this could result in companies having to accept lower profits or even having to close down. So for the time being voluntary regulation is the best we can hope for – for example, see The Year Out Group, Fairtrade Volunteering and Ethical Volunteering.

Pre-acceptance interviews and pre-departure training are essential to effectively match volunteers' skills to appropriate projects. Volunteers should also be briefed so that their expectations are realistic and they are clear about what they will be doing, where their money is going, and what they can really contribute. Organisations should actively encourage volunteers to question why global differences occur rather than just accepting them.

Despite the obvious weaknesses of volunteer tourism, it can work – if volunteers have skills that the host requires, if they go for a significant length of time, and if the communities involved have a voice in developing and managing projects. In these cases it can act as a major force for development. Unfortunately, volunteer tourism in its current structure does not address real need. It has been shaped and driven by what tourists want.

19 August 2010

➪ The above information is reprinted with kind permission from the International Institute for Environment and Development. Visit www.iied.org for more information.

© *International Institute for Environment and Development*

A volunteer's perspective on the growth in 'voluntourism'

With the growing popularity of volunteer travel, some have questioned what motivations lie behind these trips and whether they do more harm than good.

However, for a volunteer like Rebecca Boteler, volunteering abroad with the right motivation and organisation makes the experience infinitely worthwhile.

Despite long hours, challenging working conditions and no pay, Rebecca found it hugely rewarding to teach English in Cambodia.

'After zipping around the world a couple of times over the years, I'd had enough of sitting by pools sipping cocktails with those cute little umbrellas in them. I wanted to be a part of the communities I was in and help to make them better places.'

Despite long hours, challenging working conditions and no pay, Rebecca found it hugely rewarding to teach English in Cambodia

While Rebecca recognises the diverse range of people who volunteer, on a recent trip to a conservation project in Thailand she was struck by the number and commitment of gap year volunteers.

'I was surprised by their level of dedication to the animals and their ability to tough it out in rough conditions without complaining.'

Though Rebecca has harboured doubts as to the benefits of the growth in 'voluntourism' she concludes that ethical volunteer organisations make the industry worthwhile.

'And at the end of the day, seeing the benefits of my work still makes me believe I'm doing more good than harm.'

21 January 2011

➪ The above information is reprinted with kind permission from Inspire Volunteer. Visit www.inspirevolunteer.co.uk for more information.

© *Inspire Volunteer*

INTERNATIONAL INSTITUTE FOR ENVIRONMENT AND DEVELOPMENT / INSPIRE VOLUNTEER

The ethical volunteering guide

Seven questions to help you pick an ethical international volunteering placement.

By Kate Simpson

Your guide to ethical volunteering

International volunteering can be a wonderful way to explore another country, meet new people, learn new things and have new adventures.

It is now possible to find organisations providing volunteer placements in almost any corner of the world. But are all these projects really worth your time or your money? Are they doing any good – or more harm than good?

This is your guide to the questions to ask, and the answers to look for, as you try to pick between the great opportunities and the great opportunists waiting for you out there.

Get the most, give the most

People who volunteer generally hope to do something they will find interesting, something they will learn from and something that will help other people. However, choosing between all the possible projects and organisations is more complex than just signing up

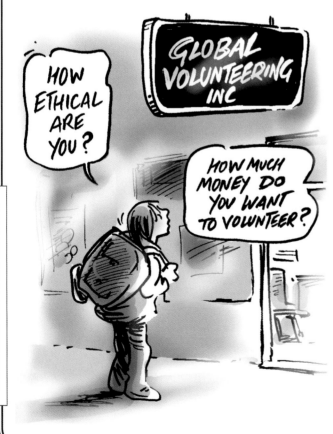

with the first one to show you exciting pictures and an interesting blurb.

To get the most out of international volunteering you need to put effort into choosing who you go with and what you do. For while there are some fantastic projects to take part in, there are also those that are poorly organised and exploit both hosts' and travellers' expectations.

These seven questions are designed to help you learn as much as possible about the quality and value of the projects or placements an organisation offers BEFORE you arrive in the country with your newly-packed backpack and a whole bundle of expectations.

Exactly what work will I be doing?

Can the organisation provide a brief job description? An organisation with a good volunteer programme should be able to tell you exactly what you will be doing, including how many hours a day, how many days a week and what sort of work it will be. For example, if an organisation offers a placement in a school, this may or may not be teaching. Likewise, a placement may involve 50 hours a week or – and this does happen – a mere four. The greatest source of dissatisfaction for volunteers usually comes from not doing what they planned (and paid) to do.

Does the organisation work with a local partner organisation?

If a volunteer programme is to be of value to a local community it should work with, rather than be imposed on, that community. High-value programmes will have been built in collaboration with a local partner organisation. Find out who that partner is and find out about the relationship. Key things to look for are whether someone from the local organisation is involved in the day-to-day management of your project, what sort of consultation went into building that project, and why the project is of value.

Does the organisation make any financial contribution to its volunteer programmes? If so, exactly how much?

Many volunteer organisations charge a lot of money, but where does it go? Volunteer programmes need funds as well as people to do the work; indeed, in much of the world, unskilled labour is one thing of which there is little shortage. The most important thing is that your organisation is up front about how your money is spent. So ask where your pennies are going, and be persistent about getting a clear figure, not a percentage of profits. Also, be aware that payments for your own food and lodging often do not assist your volunteer programme.

Does the organisation have policies on eco and ethical tourism? If so, how are they implemented?

Running volunteer programmes is ethically complex. If you really want to make a valuable contribution to the community you work with, then you have a responsibility to ensure that the organisation with which you travel has proper eco and ethical policies. Look for organisations that have a long-term commitment to a community, employ local staff and have some mechanism for local consultation and decision-making. Otherwise, how do you know that the clinic you built is really needed? That an adult literacy programme is not more relevant than a new bridge? Or that when you have left, there will be the funds and commitment to maintain the project on which you have worked?

What time frame is the volunteer programme run on?

A well-structured volunteer programme should have a clear time frame, and organisations should know from one year to the next whether a programme will continue. Programmes, and especially placements, that occur just once can be problematic. For example, if you are acting as an English teaching assistant for a month or two, what happens the rest of the school year? Are other volunteers sent, or is the placement simply ended? It may be very disruptive for a class, a school or an orphanage to have a constantly changing staff. Establishing the level of commitment an organisation has to a given project or placement is vital in establishing the quality, and therefore value, of that volunteer programme.

Can the organisation give you precise contact details for your chosen programme?

Organisations tend to work in one of two ways. The better ones build a relationship with a host organisation, identify local needs they can meet, arrange placements and projects and then fill the vacancies. A less positive approach is to wait for travellers to sign up and pay up, and then find relevant placements. A good organisation with well-run programmes should be able to let you know several months before you travel where you will be going and what exactly you will be doing. If they cannot, or will not, give you these details then be very wary of the quality of the programme. Hastily-arranged programmes can be disorganised, leaving both volunteers and local hosts with unclear expectations.

What support and training will you receive?

Organisations offer vastly different levels of training and support. Look for an organisation that offers not only pre-departure training, but also in-country training and support. As a volunteer you want to be as much use as possible, learn as much as possible and have as good a time as possible. Training in both the practicalities of your volunteer job and the culture of where you are travelling will help you get and give the most. Local support is also important. The type of programme you are on affects the amount of support required, but make sure you know what to expect before you go. If there is a local representative, how 'local' are they – just down the road, or several hours away by bus? Make sure there is somebody in the country with direct responsibility for you. All projects require some problem-solving at some point and you will need someone on hand to help you with this.

Are all these projects really worth your time or your money? Are they doing any good – or more harm than good?

⇨ The above information is reprinted with kind permission from Ethical Volunteering. Visit www. ethicalvolunteering.org for more information.

© *Ethical Volunteering*

ETHICAL VOLUNTEERING

⇨ The UK is the sixth most-visited destination by international tourists but is losing market share. (page 1)

⇨ The Internet is seen as a safe way to book travel more often than not, with more agreeing (45%) than disagreeing (18%). (page 3)

⇨ Tourism is the UK's highest export earner behind Chemicals and Financial Services. In most years it is the fifth or sixth biggest sector of the economy, behind manufacturing and retail but ahead of construction. It generates £90 billion of direct business for the economy each year. (page 4)

⇨ The *Big Hospitality* survey of 5,000 British adults conducted earlier this month found that 35 per cent of respondents will be holidaying in the UK this summer, compared to 25 per cent last year. (page 5)

⇨ A year ago the average Brit was prepared to spend £1,014 per person on their main holiday, but fast forward to 2011 and this has dropped to £829. (page 6)

⇨ The most important factors for tourists choosing a holiday destination are the country's weather; its natural beauty; whether it offers value for money; the quality and warmth of the welcome which visitors receive and whether there are plenty of interesting cultural or heritage things to do while they're there. (page 11)

⇨ Three million pounds from the Olympic budget is to be used to boost domestic tourism in 2012 and beyond, in a drive to maximise the economic legacy of the London Games for the whole country. (page 13)

⇨ One of the most controversial types of travel involves tours of vast urban slums in places like Rio de Janeiro, Soweto, Mumbai, Manila, Cairo and Mexico City. (page 16)

⇨ 'Glamping' or upmarket camping is certainly experiencing a boom, becoming more widespread and more varied. (page 20)

⇨ Over the past six decades, tourism has expanded to become one of the largest and fastest-growing economic sectors in the world. Many new destinations have emerged alongside the traditional ones of Western Europe and North America. (page 21)

⇨ One of the most obvious concerns with tourism today is its impact on climate change, through the carbon footprint in air travel. The Ecumencial Coalition on Tourism estimates that tourism's share in global warming is up to 12.5%. (page 22)

⇨ Ecotourism has to be both ecologically and socially conscious. Its goal is to minimise the impact that tourism has on an area through cooperation and management and in some cases it even encourages travellers to have a positive impact on their new surroundings. (page 24)

⇨ Massive influxes of tourists, often to a relatively small area, have a huge impact. They add to the pollution, waste, and water needs of the local population, putting local infrastructure and habitats under enormous pressure. (page 25)

⇨ Wildlife tourism can have a role to play in stopping detrimental activities by increasing awareness and encouraging people to relish rather than ravish the natural environment. (page 26)

⇨ Mass-tourism expenses for all-inclusive packages hardly ever reach the natives since they pay for airlines, hotels, guides and other international companies. (page 28)

⇨ The voluntary tourism sector is now largely driven by the market and the demands of tourists, so host communities have little power over how things are developed, managed and run. They rarely have a say in what happens where and why. (page 36)

⇨ Despite the obvious weaknesses of volunteer tourism, it can work – if volunteers have skills that the host requires, if they go for a significant length of time, and if the communities involved have a voice in developing and managing projects. (page 37)

Alternative tourism

Any form of tourism that differs from the 'mass market': for example, tornado chasing, couch surfing or visiting sites of natural disasters, as opposed to beach or package holidays.

Couch surfing

Couch surfing originally referred to the practice of staying on friends' sofas when in need of accommodation. More recently, the definition has expanded and some budget travellers now 'couch surf' for free with strangers in order to reduce travel costs and meet new people.

Domestic tourism

Residents holidaying within their own country, for example Britons who holiday in Cornwall.

Ecotourism

Ecotourism is closely related to 'responsible tourism' and generally refers to a form of travel that is conscious of preserving both the ecology and the local culture/community of a tourist destination.

GDP (gross domestic product)

Gross Domestic Product refers to the value of all the products and services produced by a country within a certain time period.

Glamping

Glamping refers to up-market, 'glamorous' camping.

Global footprint

A person's global footprint refers to the impact that they have on the planet and the people around them, taking into account how much land and water each person needs to sustain their lifestyle.

Green tourism

The concept of green tourism is very similar to 'ecotourism'. Green tourism involves thinking about how you reach your destination (for example, taking public transport instead of driving) as well as the impact you have on the local environment once you arrive.

Greenwashing

'Greenwashing' occurs when organisations falsely promote or market themselves as having 'green', environmentally-friendly, practices.

Homestay

A homestay is a form of travel accommodation in which tourists pay to live with a local family instead of staying in a hotel. This form of accommodation is considered to be extremely eco-friendly, and is often used by volunteer programmes. Meals are often included.

Poverty tourism

Poverty tourism refers to the practice of visiting extremely poor areas or communities in search of an 'authentic' experience. Poverty tourism often involves 'slum tours', in which tourists are led around sites such as the Favellas of Rio di Janeiro or taken to visit the street children of Delhi.

Socio-economic

Concerning both social and economic factors.

Sustainable tourism

Sustainable tourism is closely linked to ecotourism and involves having as little impact as possible on local ecosystems and communities when visiting a destination. Sustainable tourists may choose to travel by rail instead of air, for example, and support local businesses instead of international companies.

Voluntourism

Tourism which includes volunteer work as part of the tour or holiday experience. This is becoming increasingly popular, especially with gap year travellers. Examples include teaching English to children or carrying out environmental projects.

ACKNOWLEDGEMENTS

The publisher is grateful for permission to reproduce the following material.

While every care has been taken to trace and acknowledge copyright, the publisher tenders its apology for any accidental infringement or where copyright has proved untraceable. The publisher would be pleased to come to a suitable arrangement in any such case with the rightful owner.

Chapter One: Travel Trends

Overseas visitors to Britain, © VisitBritain, *Why tourism matters,* © Crown Copyright is reproduced with the permission of Her Majesty's Stationery Office, *Britons to spend £7 billion on home holidays this summer,* © Big Hospitality, *Brits will spend a fifth less on 2011 holidays,* © TravelSupermarket.com, *Planes, trains and smartphones: trends affecting adventure travel in 2011,* © Adventure Travel Trade Association, *Travel health advice from Dr Felicity Nicholson, Trailfinders Travel Clinic,* © Clasado, *Is Britain an attractive tourism destination?,* © Crown Copyright is reproduced with the permission of Her Majesty's Stationery Office, *£3 million from Olympic budget to boost domestic tourism in 2012 and beyond,* © Crown Copyright is reproduced with the permission of Her Majesty's Stationery Office, *Ukinbound warns against Olympic 'misperceptions',* © Ukinbound, *Raising air passenger duty flight tax will hurt UK tourism, Osborne told,* © Telegraph Media Group Limited 2011, *Foreign Office releases figures on Brits in trouble overseas,* © Crown copyright is reproduced with the permission of Her Majesty's Stationery Office, *Five types of alternative tourism,* © HotelClub Travel Blog, *Brits for blast off: tourists head to final frontier,* © Telegraph Media Group Limited 2011, *South Africa – top destination for structured gap year programmes,* © Year Out Group, *Glamping – camping at its best,* © International Tourism Trade Fairs Association.

Chapter Two: Sustainability and Ethics

Sustainable tourism, © The World Bank, *Case study – the Maldives: lost in paradise,* © Humanities Education Centre, *What is ecotourism?,* © i-to-i, *Coastal development problems: tourism,* © WWF Global, *Can wildlife tourism help conserve our endangered species?,* © Responsible travel.com, *'Green people' in global tourism – a new way to travel,* © Earth Times, *How your travels will affect local communities,* © i-to-i, *Integrating ethics into tourism: beyond codes of conduct,* © Guardian News and Media Limited 2011, *Amazon town bans tourists,* © Guardian News and Media Limited 2011, *Slumming it,* © The Oxonian Globalist, *Responsible tourism,* © Crown copyright is reproduced with the permission of Her Majesty's Stationery Office, *Volunteer tourism defies recession but is this positive news for the South?,* © International Institute for Environment and Development, *A volunteer's perspective on the growth in 'voluntourism',* © Inspire Volunteer, *The ethical volunteering guide,* © Ethical Volunteering.

Illustrations

Pages 3, 6, 12, 38: Simon Kneebone; pages 9, 21, 28, 39: Angelo Madrid; pages 10, 18, 23, 30: Don Hatcher; pages 14, 27: Bev Aisbett.

Cover photography

Left: © Jenny w. Centre: © JohnNyberg, sxc.hu. Right: © Bert van 't Hul.

Additional acknowledgements

Editorial by Carolyn Kirby on behalf of Independence.

With thanks to the Independence team: Mary Chapman, Sandra Dennis and Jan Sunderland.

Lisa Firth
Cambridge
January, 2012

ASSIGNMENTS

The following tasks aim to help you think through the debate surrounding tourism and provide a better understanding of the topic.

1 In groups, imagine that you have been asked to develop a new television advertisement which will encourage international tourists to visit Britain. Think about why people visit the UK; what are the most popular tourist attractions? VisitBritain's *Overseas visitors to Britain* report on page 1 indicates that 70% of people choose holiday destinations based on natural scenic beauty, so try to include some descriptions and images of areas known for this characteristic, such as the Lake District. Create a storyboard which shows your advertisement scene by scene, including details of any soundtracks you plan to use or celebrities you want to appear.

2 TripAdvisor and Wikipedia have both created travel apps for smartphones. Come up with your own proposal for a new travel app. Think about consumer behaviour, and consider what useful features you would want to include. Compare your app with other students in your class: whose would you choose to purchase?

3 Read *Five types of alternative tourism* on page 16. In groups, choose one of the five types and create a presentation to convince the other groups that your chosen type of tourism is the most exciting. You should include details of sample destinations and may use PowerPoint to help you if you wish. Try to include facts, photos and reviews to help promote your chosen type of tourism.

4 Domestic tourism is becoming more popular in the UK, with increasing numbers of Britons choosing to holiday in their own country rather than abroad. Think about places close to you and why they might be good locations for a holiday. Look into details of local accommodation, activities and interesting sights, then design a tourist brochure based on your findings.

5 '"Voluntourism" is at best tokenism, and at worst exploitation of local people'. To what extent do you think this statement is fair? Discuss this statement in small groups. What conclusions do you draw?

6 Read *£3 million from Olympic budget to boost domestic tourism in 2012 and beyond* on page 12 and *Ukinbound warns against Olympic 'misperceptions'* on page 13. The two articles present differing views of the 2012 Olympic Games. Write a critical evaluation of the two articles, comparing and contrasting their arguments. Why do you think they present such different opinions?

7 Imagine you are travelling to Vietnam on a backpacking holiday. Starting with the Foreign Office website, investigate the advice given to tourists on how they should prepare for travel to Vietnam. Consider sources such as Lonely Planet or Rough Guides, but also take a look at any travel blogs or forums that you come across. Is the advice consistent and straightforward? Write a summary of your findings.

8 Using newspapers and the Internet, research a tourist destination of your choice and evaluate the positive and negative effects of tourism on that location. How can tourism to this area be made more responsible and sustainable?

9 Investigate three different volunteer-based holidays which are available. Look at where the placements are, what they entail, how much they cost and how much support is offered. Do you think these holidays could be classed as 'responsible' travel? Write a summary of your findings.

10 Do you think that space tourism will continue to develop? Is Richard Branson's Virgin Galactic the start of a new trend in tourism? Role play an item on a breakfast chat show discussing the issue of space tourism. One student should play the role of the host, and other students can play travel industry experts and tourists arguing either for or against space travel as the 'next big thing'.

11 In pairs, choose a holiday destination. You should each research how much a four-night trip to your chosen destination would cost for two adults. However, one of you should make your holiday 'green' and the other 'mainstream'. Make sure you report a breakdown of costs: for example, accommodation and flights. Compare your findings with your partner's. Is 'green' travel more expensive?

12 'It is unfair that a gap year is considered to enhance a CV and make someone more attractive to employers when only the well-off can afford the luxury of a year travelling. It is a form of indirect discrimination against the less well-off.' Do you think this is a fair statement? Discuss your views in small groups. The graphs on page 19 provide some statistics you could quote in your discussion.